L. A. LEGEND

By

Aaron Denius

To my first two writing buddies, Oren and Todd. I still remember the late-night writing sessions we used to have at the Hillel, where a good majority of my earlier scripts were written. It was also fun breaking the rules by ordering non-Kosher pizza. Your creativity helped set me on a path to discovering my passion for writing. Without those earlier days, I would not be where I am today. I am eternally grateful.

FOREWORD

A brief history of "L.A. Legend"

I'm pretty sure I was possessed when I wrote "L.A. Legend". I couldn't really tell you how the idea came to mind, I just started writing and 21 days later I had a completed screenplay. I remember listening to the debut album of Scissor Sisters on repeat in order to keep my mental momentum. Now, any time I hear a song from that album I have a Pavlovian response and the writing bug gets me.

After a few rounds of editing, I began entering the screenplay into various competitions. Though it never won any (I don't think contests want winning scripts that have the word 'fuck' in it over 100 times), the screenplay placed as a semi-finalist or finalist in nearly all competitions. The judges were comparing "L.A. Legend" to "Pulp Fiction", "The Usual Suspects", and "Rashomon".

All these accolades certainly got me excited about the prospects of this screenplay and my writing future. Production companies were taking notice and the script was optioned multiple times – An option is when a production company pays you to hold the exclusive rights to the script in order for them to secure financing, attach actors and bring on a studio. For every 1,000 optioned scripts, maybe 1 gets turned in to a movie.

Each option I had progressed through various stages. Some fell through at the financing stage. Others were in negotiations with actors, including one with an actress, which the production company had me re-write the entire script for a female lead (I'll admit, it wasn't as good). The most heartbreaking one was an option that seemed to have the most promise but was abruptly ended when the Writer's Guild went on strike. After the strike ended, the momentum was killed and the production company moved on to another project.

Hollywood can be a bitch that way. You certainly need to have tough skin if you want to work in the industry. I continued writing and seemed to pay less attention to "L.A. Legend", feeling it had run its course. A couple of years passed and then I was approached with an opportunity to work on a TV show. I had to submit a sample and I chose "L.A. Legend" as I felt it was the best fit. A week later I got a call to meet with the showrunner and was then offered the job. A couple of years later the show was cancelled, but I would not have had that opportunity if it were not for this script.

It has now been a couple of years since that show and I feel that this script shouldn't just sit on my desktop, gathering virtual dust. I want to share it, offer an insight to a screenplay that gets attention, but for one reason or another doesn't get made into a film. At the very least some people who would otherwise never see it, will get a chance to enjoy reading the story!

EXT. DOWNTOWN LOS ANGELES - DAY

A beat-up red Ford Escort speeds along city streets
with no regard for traffic lights or stop signs.

Three unmarked police cars, a few souped-up gangster
cars, and four black SUV's chase the Escort. The
cars swerve in and out of traffic, leaving chaos
behind them.

I/E. RED FORD ESCORT - DAY

MAINE RICHTER, late 20's, drives frantically through
downtown. He looks at his mirrors to check the cars
behind him.

He makes a sharp turn and heads up a street where
KIDS play on the sidewalks. A young KID jumps on a
pogo stick across the street.

The kid stalls in the middle and stares at Maine as
the car inches closer.

                    MAINE
          Get off the road!

Maine swerves as he frantically waves the kid off
the road. The kid attempts to clear the road, but
trips and falls over his pogo stick.

                    MAINE
          Damn it!

Maine slams on the brakes. He jumps out of the car
and runs over to the kid.

                    MAINE
          Are you okay?

                    KID
          I think you broke my leg.

                   MAINE
              Sorry.

Maine grabs the kid by his arms and drags him to the
sidewalk. He runs back to his car, as a black SUV
speeds closer.

                    KID
              Asshole!

Maine steps on the gas, leaving a small cloud of
smoke. The SUV hits the Escort's back bumper and the
passengers of the SUV shoot at Maine.

He peeks back at the kid to confirm his safety and
doesn't notice the large wooden ramp ahead of him.
He looks forward, panics, and turns the wheel
sharply.

                   MAINE
              Shit!

The left wheels of the car hit the ramp, forcing the
car to swerve through some trashcans.

Behind him, the SUV heads directly for the ramp.
Maine checks the side-view mirror. The SUV smashes
through the wood.

Maine looks forward and sees the 10 freeway straight
ahead. He takes the on ramp and heads west.

The cars following him form a single-file line and
enter the freeway. The freeway is surprisingly
barren. The cars form a pack across all the lanes
behind the red Escort.

Maine looks at the rear-view mirror, then straight
into the camera.

                    MAINE
          My name is Maine Richter, and
          this is how I became the most
          wanted man in L.A.
                    (beat)
          So books, check it out. About a
          week ago, I get a call from my
          brother.

INT. MAINE'S APARTMENT - AFTERNOON

Maine sits at his kitchen table eating a bowl of
children's cereal, watching an episode of "The
Simpsons". Overdue bills and notices scatter the
table.

He finishes the cereal and slurps the milk from the
bowl. His eyes never leave the TV.

                    MAINE
          "Hello, Mr. Burns. This is your
          mother, Mrs. Burns". Hehe.

Maine takes the bowl to the sink. The phone rings.
Maine picks it up, keeping his eyes on the TV.

                    MAINE
          Hello?

                    RYLAND   (V.O.)
          Hey Maine.

                    MAINE
          Ryland how's it going?

                    RYLAND   (V.O.)
          You sitting down?

Maine grabs an apple from the counter. He takes a
bite.

                    MAINE
          Yeah, what's up?

                    RYLAND   (V.O.)
          I got cancer.

Maine chuckles at the TV, and then realizes what his
brother said. The apple falls from his mouth.

                    MAINE
          What?!

He turns off the TV and sits down.

                    RYLAND   (V.O.)
          The doctor said I have cancer. I
          need chemo.

                    MAINE
          How did...

                    RYLAND   (V.O.)
          I don't know man.

                    MAINE
          Do you have ins...

                    RYLAND   (V.O.)
          No insurance, and I sure as hell
          don't got the money.

                    MAINE
          Fuck.

                    RYLAND   (V.O.)
          Yeah.

Maine lays his head on the table, the phone pressed
to his ear.

                    RYLAND
          Kind of ironic don't you think?

                    MAINE
          What?

                    RYLAND (V.O.)
          Cancer. I mean I always thought I
          would get shot or stabbed or
          something.

Maine lifts his head and a smile cracks his face.

                    MAINE
          You know Ryland, you are an
          idiot. Why do you always turn
          things into a joke?

                    RYLAND (V.O.)
          What can I say? I'm just talented
          that way.

                    MAINE
          Listen, we'll get the money
          somehow. I'll work extra shifts
          if I have to.

                    RYLAND (V.O.)
          You're the best bro. Hey I gotta
          go, but let's take a trip soon.

                    MAINE
          Sounds good. Later.

Maine hangs up.

INT. MAINE'S APARTMENT, BATHROOM - NIGHT

Maine has a towel around his waist and brushes his
teeth. He leans close into the mirror and looks at a
blemish on his face.

                    MAINE (V.O.)
          Then, five days later...

Maine wanders over to the bathroom window. He looks
out to see a man wearing a light blue baseball cap
breaking into his car.

                    MAINE
              That's my car!!!

Toothpaste sprays all over the window and dribbles
down his chin. The man gets into the car and turns
it on. Maine runs out of the bathroom towards the
front door.

                    MAINE
              Fuck!

The towel slips off his body and falls to the ground
as Maine opens his door.

TWO OLD WOMEN chat in the hallway a few doors down.
Maine stands at the doorway naked, shocked to see
the old women.

                    OLD WOMAN 1
              ...can you believe that whore
              didn't show up for bridge.

The old women look at Maine.

                    OLD WOMAN 2
              Hello Maine.

                    MAINE
              Hey.

                    OLD WOMAN 1
              You looking for some action young
              man?

Maine looks down at his naked body.

                    OLD WOMAN 2
              Agnes, behave.
                        (beat)
              I saw him first.

The old women smile at Maine as he slams the door.

6

He runs back to the bathroom and looks out the
window to find his car gone. Maine sits on the
toilet with his head in his hands.

                    MAINE
          Damn it!

Maine's cell phone rings. He reaches down into his
crumpled pants on the floor and pulls out his cell
phone.

                    MAINE
          Yeah?

                    RYLAND (V.O.)
          It's Ryland. Quick question.
          Think you can still street race?

                    MAINE
          What? Yeah. Why?

                    RYLAND (V.O.)
          Cool, I'll call you back later.

Ryland hangs up.

                    MAINE
          Cool?! What? Ahhhh!

Maine stares at his phone confused, and then angrily
punches his shower curtain. He plops down onto the
bathroom floor and dials on his phone.

                    OPERATOR
          911. What's your emergency?

                    MAINE
          I'd like to report a car theft.

EXT. STARBUCKS/STREET - DAY

An empty, quiet street in front of Starbucks.

                    MAINE   (V.O.)
          The next day, today, I reached my
          final straw.

Maine storms out of the Starbucks wearing a green
apron.

                    MAINE   (V.O.)
          Without a car, I was late. Very
          late. And I might have been just
          a little emotional about my
          brother.

Maine turns and flips off the store with both hands.

                    MAINE
          Fuck you, your mother, and your
          grandmother, you piece of shit. I
          don't need you!

He rips off the green apron, tries to take bite out
of it, and throws it at the window.

                    MAINE
               Assholes.

Maine storms away and checks his watch. He walks a
couple of blocks mumbling to himself. He turns a
corner and freezes.

A half a block down is his car, idling on the side
of the road. He looks around, and quietly walks
towards the car.

No one is in the car and the engine hums quietly.

                    MAINE
          He left the fucker running.

Maine walks to the driver's side, not noticing the man with the light blue baseball cap, RICH, late 20's, urinating in a nook of the building.

Maine jumps into the car and speeds away. Rich, who hasn't finished, turns to see the car peeling out.

                    RICH
          Oh shit!

Rich runs after the car, to no avail.

                    RICH
             Wait!! Come back. Damn it!

Rich looks down at the small wet spot on his ridiculously baggy pants.

                    RICH
             Fucking genius.

He zips up and waddles away.

INT. RED FORD ESCORT - CONTINUOUS

Maine grips the steering wheel tightly as a heavy metal song screams through the radio. On the seat next to him are an empty soda cup, a wallet, and a crumpled blanket.

                    MAINE (V.O.)
             Of course, my luck got worse.

Maine looks in the rear-view mirror. No one is behind him, but in the bottom of the rear-view something catches his attention.

He turns around to see 15 large burlap sacks with hundred-dollar bills poking out.

                    MAINE
          Oh fuck!

Main pulls the car to the side of the road and
stares in awe at the money. A knock at the passenger
window startles him. It's a beautiful girl, MEGAN,
20's. She wears a tight workout outfit and an iPod.

> MAINE
>> Shit, shit, shit.

Maine thinks quickly and throws the blanket over the
money. He then leans across and opens the door from
the inside.

> MEGAN
> You know a real gentleman would
> get out of the car to open the
> door.

Megan gets into the car and kisses Maine. He faints
a kiss back and drives.

> MAINE
> Hi Megan.

> MEGAN
> I haven't heard from you in a
> couple of days. Why haven't you
> called?

> MAINE
> Um, yeah, there's been a lot of
> shit going on. I don't really
> want to talk about it.
>> (beat)
> What are you doing over here?

> MEGAN
> I was on my way to visit you at
> work.
>> (beat)
> Why aren't you at work?

> MAINE
> I uh...well.

                    MEGAN
          You need to get a career Maine.
          You are at a dead-end job. I
          can't be with someone who isn't
          goal driven.

Maine constantly checks his rear-view.

                    MEGAN
          Are you even listening to me?!

                    MAINE
          Huh? Oh...Yeah...

Maine drives the car slowly, when suddenly he spots
three black cars behind him.

One of the black cars places a light on its roof and
flashes its lights at Maine.

                    MAINE
          Fuck! Sorry Megan.

Maine peels out and the three black cars chase after
him.

                    MEGAN
          Maine, what the hell are you
          doing?

                    MAINE
          I don't know.

                    MEGAN
          What do you mean you don't know?
          Those are cops. You have to stop.

                    MAINE
          I can't. I...damn it.

                    MEGAN
          What?!

                    MAINE
          Look in the back seat.

Megan turns and lifts up a corner of the blanket.
She notices the bags of money and screams.

                    MEGAN
          What the hell did you do?!

                    MAINE
          Nothing. I didn't do anything.

                    MEGAN
          Then why is there like twenty
          million dollars in your back
          seat?

                    MAINE
          Twenty million? You really think
          it's that much?

                    MEGAN
          I don't care. But you better
          explain why you have all that
          money in your back seat.

                    MAINE
          Or what? You won't talk to me?

Megan shoots Maine a look.

                    MEGAN
          Don't be an ass.

                    MAINE
          Fine. Sorry. Well, I told you my
          car was stolen right?

Maine makes a hard right and speeds away from the
black cars.

                    MEGAN
          No, you didn't. See this is what
          I'm talking about. You don't tell
          me anything. Dr. Phil says that
          couples need...

                    MAINE
          Are you going to let me tell you
          what happened?

Megan stares daggers at Maine. A few souped-up
gangster cars join in the chase.

                    MAINE
          So, my car had been stolen. I
          called the police and reported it.
          They said they would do what they
          could to recover it.

                    MEGAN
          So, they did?

                    MAINE
          No. I'm getting there. So, I was
          fired from my job this morning.

                    MEGAN
          And again, I'm just hearing this
          now.

                    MAINE
          It just fucking happened!

                    MEGAN
          Whatever.

                    MAINE
          So, I'm walking away from the
          Starbucks, when I see my car idling
          on the street.

                    MEGAN
          You stole a car!

                    MAINE
          It's my fucking car! What am I
          supposed to do?!

                    MEGAN
          I don't know...So when did you get
          the money?

                    MAINE
          It was in the car.

                    MEGAN
          So why did you speed away when the
          cops came up behind you?

                    MAINE
          I don't know, I panicked, they
          would probably think I stole it.
          Besides, how do you know they are
          cops?

                    MEGAN
          The lights.

                    MAINE   -
          I mean they could be bad cops or
          the mob or something.

                    MEGAN
          Really? The mob? Please don't
          patronize me.

                    MAINE
          Well, you explain why there are
          more people chasing us?

Megan looks behind at the cars chasing them and
freaks out.

                    MEGAN
          Let me out. Pull over.

                         MAINE
          What? You don't think they would
          pull over and take you and hold you
          for ransom or something?

                         MEGAN
          Well I...Maine watch out!!!

                         MAINE
          Fuck!

A black SUV pulls out in front of the Escort and
stops in their way. Maine turns the wheel hard,
narrowly missing a collision.

He speeds down a street with speed bumps. Maine
tries to speed over the first bump. The car goes
slightly airborne. A loud clank sounds as the car
lands back on the ground.

                         MEGAN
          What was that clank?

                         MAINE
          The engine?

                         MEGAN
          Well, that's not a surprise with
          this piece of shit.

                         MAINE
          I was kidding.

Maine slows up slightly for the next bumps as 4
black SUV's join the chase.

                         MEGAN
          There are SUV's chasing us now!

                         MAINE
          Now that's probably the mob.

MEGAN
What?! I can't believe you got me
into this.

Megan crouches down in her seat, scared.

INT. UNCLE FESTER'S SHOWER - MORNING

ANTHONY "UNCLE FESTER" NISTA, Italian, late 40's,
washes himself in his shower. He looks just like his
nickname. His shower is lavish with gold engraving.

TWO WOMEN in bikinis stand holding a towel and a
robe. Uncle Fester loudly sings "O Sole Mio". The
two girls giggle.

UNCLE FESTER
(singing)
Ma n'atu sole. Cchiu bello, oje ne.
'O sole mio. Sta 'nfronte a te!

CHYRON: "ANTHONY 'UNCLE FESTER' NISTA"

INT. CATHOLIC CHURCH - DAY

Uncle Fester walks in to a glorious Catholic Church.
He kneels at the start of the pews and crosses
himself.

He proceeds to the confessional booth and sits in.
The slide door opens, revealing the bottom portion
of FATHER RICO'S face.

UNCLE FESTER
Forgive me Father, for I have
sinned.

FATHER RICO
Speak my son, and the Lord will
listen.

Uncle Fester leans closer to the slide door.

16

                    UNCLE FESTER
         I've had impure thoughts about a
         woman other than my wife.

                    FATHER RICO
         The Lord forgives...

                    UNCLE FESTER
         It was a busty blonde. Her tits
         were flawless. As if two angels
         filled her bra...

                    FATHER RICO
         Sir, this is highly inappropriate.

                    UNCLE FESTER
         Why, Father? Is it turning you on?

Father Rico looks through the slide door.

                    FATHER RICO
         Anthony, is that you?

                    UNCLE FESTER
         In the flesh.

                    FATHER RICO
         You asshole!

                    UNCLE FESTER
         I was turning you on, wasn't I?

                    FATHER RICO
         I was just...

                    UNCLE FESTER
         Do you touch yourself in there, you
         pervert? Man, you need help.

                    FATHER RICO
         You want to hear what I got or not?

                    UNCLE FESTER
          I'm all ears.

                    FATHER RICO
          Two weeks ago, Royal America Bank
          filed for bankruptcy... They are
          moving all their funds to one bank
          for holding while they transition.

                    UNCLE FESTER
          What bank?

                    FATHER RICO
          I don't know, but they will be
          moving all the money to their
          affiliate back east in two weeks.

                    UNCLE FESTER
          How do you know...

                    FATHER RICO
          Royal America was the church's
          bank.

                    UNCLE FESTER
          Rico, what would I do without you?

                    FATHER RICO
          I owe you my life Anthony. I help
          when I can.

Uncle Fester exits the confessional and crosses
himself again before he leaves the church.

EXT. CATHOLIC CHURCH - CONTINUOUS

Uncle Fester waits at the sidewalk and dials his
cell phone.

                    BOSLEY (V.O.)
          Hello?

                    UNCLE FESTER
          Bosley, it's Nista. I'm calling in
          that favor you owe me.

                    BOSLEY   (V.O.)
          Go on...

                    UNCLE FESTER
          A shit load of money is being
          transferred to one bank in L.A. I
          need to know which one...

A limousine stops in front of Uncle Fester and he
gets in.

EXT. BACK ALLEY - EVENING

CHYRON: 8 DAYS LATER

EDDIE, white, 20's, is tied up next to a dumpster.
Eddie bleeds from every orifice of his body.

Surrounding him are six guys in nicely pressed
suits.

CHO, Asian, late 20's, built like a castle. The new
guy.

MARRICK, white, late 30's, a skinny balding man
obsessed with combing his remaining hair.

KATZ, Jewish, early 20's, with a red afro and two
scars across his entire face that create an "X".

YAR, white, 50's, with an eye patch and a short
white Mohawk. Yar eats out of a bag of cat food.

MEASLES, Italian, late 40's, with red splotches on
his skin. He stands next to his boss and cousin,
Uncle Fester.

                    UNCLE FESTER
          Cho, don't you need to piss?

                    CHO
          No.

Uncle Fester points to Eddie.

                    UNCLE FESTER
          Take a leak on Eddie. Will you do
          that for me Cho.

                    CHO
          But I don't gotta...

Uncle Fester points a gun at Cho.

                    CHO
          Okay, okay. I'll go.

Cho gives Eddie a smirk and removes his jacket. He
hands his jacket to Katz and walks over to Eddie,
unzipping his pants.

                    UNCLE FESTER
          So, Eddie, are you gonna tell us
          what bank the money is being
          stored?

Eddie stays silent and stares at Cho.

                    UNCLE FESTER
          Cho, will you go already?

                    CHO
          I can't. I need some water.

                    UNCLE FESTER
          Are you shitting me? Marrick, go
          kick him in the groin, see if that
          helps.

Marrick puts his comb away and walks over towards
Cho, lifting up his pant leg.

                    CHO
          NO! Wait stop. It's coming, it's
          coming.

Uncle Fester waves Marrick back. Marrick takes his
comb out and slicks his "hair" back.

                 UNCLE FESTER
          So, Eddie, what's it gonna be?

Eddie stays silent, when from his side a small urine
stream hits him on the cheek. Eddie recoils in
disgust.

                    KATZ
          That's it?

                    CHO
          Shut up Katz.

Instantly a steady stream of urine pours out of Cho
and onto Eddie. Eddie vomits and curls up covering
his face.

Cho squirts the last few dribbles and then zips up
as he walks back to retrieve his jacket.

                 UNCLE FESTER
          You aren't talking Eddie; did you
          actually enjoy that?

Eddie straightens up and spits in Uncle Fester's
direction. Uncle Fester watches as the spit lands
near his shoe.

                 UNCLE FESTER
          Anyone here need to take a shit?

Yar raises his hand.

                    EDDIE
          Oh god. Alright, alright. I'll tell
          you.

Uncle Fester waves Yar back, who shrugs and eats the cat food.

                    UNCLE FESTER
          So where is it?

                    EDDIE
          First National Bank in Santa
          Monica.

                    UNCLE FESTER
          See that wasn't so bad.

Uncle Fester turns and walks towards his blacked-out SUV.

                    MEASLES
          What if he's lying?

                    CHO
          Should we kill this shmuck?

Eddie panics.

                    EDDIE
          No! I told you what you wanted.
          Don't kill me.

Uncle Fester stops and turns.

                    UNCLE FESTER
          Cho, you know that killing is
          against my religion.

The mobsters share a laugh.

                    EDDIE
          Thank you, God.

                    UNCLE FESTER
          But make sure he can't talk.

                    KATZ
          Yes sir.

Katz whips out a double-edged Samurai sword and
walks towards Eddie.

                    EDDIE
          Nooooo!!!

Katz approaches Eddie as Uncle Fester walks away.

INT. BLACK SUV - MOMENTS LATER

Uncle Fester sits on one side of the enormous back
seat, Measles sits on the other. An Italian aria
plays over the speakers.

                    UNCLE FESTER
          Get me Bosley.

Measles takes out a phone from his jacket pocket,
dials a number, and hands it to Uncle Fester.

                    MEASLES
          Anthony, what if he was lying?

                    UNCLE FESTER
          He wasn't.

                    MEASLES
          How do...

                    UNCLE FESTER
          Like our fathers used to say
          cousin. Fear exposes all cowards.

                    BOSLEY (V.O.)
          Hello?

                    UNCLE FESTER
          It's Nista.
                    (beat)
          First National in Santa Monica.

                    BOSLEY (V.O.)
          All of it?

                        UNCLE FESTER
           Yes, all of it. Be at Rosemont in
           one hour.

                        BOSLEY   (V.O.)
           Alright.

Uncle Fester hangs up the phone and hands it back to
Measles. They sit and listen to an Italian aria.

INT. ROSEMONT - LATER

HENRY, a butler with a Cajun drawl walks towards the
front door of this Malibu mansion.   THREE BUSTY
WOMEN cross his path.

                        WOMAN 1
           Hello Jeeves.

A woman pinches Henry's butt.

                        HENRY
           It's Henry ma'am.

The women walk away giggling and Henry proceeds to
the door. Henry opens the door, revealing BOSLEY,
late 30's, large and intimidating.

                        HENRY
           Mista Bosley, welcome to Rosemont.
           Mista Nista is awaitin you. Please
           follow me.

Henry closes the door and walks. Bosley follows
through the LIVING ROOM, DINING ROOM, KITCHEN and
out to...

EXT. ROSEMONT, SWIMMING POOL - CONTINUOUS

Bosley stands at the door and Henry disappears
behind him. The pool is enormous with a waterfall
and a large hot tub attached. Yar greets Bosley at
the door.

24

                    YAR
          This way.

                    BOSLEY
          And you are?

                    YAR
          Yar.

They walk over to the side of the hot tub, where a
chair and a drink await Bosley.

                    YAR
          Sit.

Bosley has a seat and drinks. Behind him, Uncle
Fester walks out from a change room wearing a robe.
Marrick and Cho follow with towels.

                    UNCLE FESTER
          Mr. Bosley. So glad you could make
          it.

Uncle Fester eases himself into the hot tub.

                    BOSLEY
          Did I have a choice?

Bosley laughs nervously.

                    UNCLE FESTER
          Of course, you did. But you might
          not have liked what would have
          happened if you didn't come.

Uncle Fester's men sit down around Bosley. Measles
is absent.

                    UNCLE FESTER
          We still have a deal, don't we?

                    BOSLEY
          Yes, we get twenty five percent.

                    UNCLE FESTER
          Actually, fifteen.

                    BOSLEY
          You said...

                    UNCLE FESTER
          I say a lot of things. Understand
          though, fifteen percent is a great
          sum of money. Near three million.

Bosley looks up in shock.

                    BOSLEY
          That means the total take is
          over...

                    UNCLE FESTER
          Yes. So, you understand why it is
          important to have it run smoothly.

                    BOSLEY
          Yes sir.

A couple of the bikini-clad girls join Uncle Fester
in the hot tub.

                    UNCLE FESTER
          You've enlisted in good men?

                    BOSLEY
          The best. You have my word. I would
          trust these men with my life.

                    UNCLE FESTER
          Excellent. I would hate to see this
          end ugly.

Katz stands up next to Bosley brandishing a large
mace. Bosley takes notice and gulps the rest of his
drink.

                    UNCLE FESTER
          Ha ha ha. Please Bosley, relax.
          Join me in the tub, have one of my
          girls. It will all be fine. I
          wouldn't use you if I couldn't
          trust you.

Cho places a towel and a bathing suit next to
Bosley. Across the pool two of the busty women wave
at him.

INT. RICH'S SHOWER - MORNING

Rich, stands in his dirty shower washing himself. He
has more ink than skin covering his body.

A cockroach runs up the wall and Rich spits some
water at it. Rich sings Ozzy Osbourne's "Crazy
Train".

                    RICH
                  (singing)
          Maybe it's not too late. To learn
          how to love, and forget how to
          hate. Mental wounds not healing.
          Life's a bitter shame.
                  (beat)
          I'm going off the rails on a crazy
          train...

He washes his hair and then reaches out of the
shower. He grabs his light blue hat and places it on
his wet head. He points the water to his body and
sings.

CHYRON: "RICH"

INT. WAREHOUSE - EVENING

Loud hip-hop music blares over the speakers, as
loads of gangsters dance, do drugs, and sleep.

Measles walks through the door and makes his way through the crowd. He bobs his head and walks to the beat, a la John Travolta in "Saturday Night Fever".

Measles pushes a few people out of the way, getting "fuck you" responses. He reaches the back of the warehouse, where Rich sits on a throne like seat.

Rich has 4 women all over him. He pushes the women off when he sees Measles.

                    RICH
          Jesus old man. What the fuck are
          you doing here? You'll get yourself
          killed.

                    MEASLES
          I doubt that.

                    RICH
          What makes you so sure?

Rich brandishes his gun.

                    MEASLES
          Because you wouldn't want to deal
          with the consequences.

Rich stares at Measles and slowly puts his gun away.

                    RICH
          You're fucking Measles, aren't you?

                    MEASLES
          Let's go somewhere quiet.

Rich gets up and Measles follows.

INT. COCAINE ROOM - CONTINUOUS

They walk into a back room where people snort
cocaine.

                    RICH
          Out. Now!

The people instantly scatter out of the room. Rich
closes the door then points to the table of cocaine.

                    RICH
          Help yourself.

                    MEASLES
          No.

Measles sits.

                    RICH
          Why are you here?

                    MEASLES
          I have a business deal for you.

Rich sits.

INT. WAREHOUSE - MOMENTS LATER

Rich opens the door, as he and Measles walk through.

                    MEASLES
          You can make yourself quite
          powerful and rich, Rich.

                    RICH
          Ha! Nice one.

                    MEASLES
          Wha?...oh.

Measles manages a slight smile, then progresses
through the crowd and out the door.

Rich whistles and instantly TWO GANGSTERS walk over and join him in the cocaine room.

                    RICH
          Fellas. I have just made an
          incredible business deal. One that
          will be very lucrative for us.

The gangsters sit.

                    RICH
          The First National Bank on Santa
          Monica got a shit load of cash, and
          this is what we are going to do.

EXT. MAINE'S APARTMENT - NIGHT

Rich walks up to Maine's car carrying a large black backpack. He opens the backpack pulls out a jimmy and slides it down the side of the door. The door unlocks and Rich opens the door.

                    MAINE (O.S.)
          That's my car!!

Rich turns and looks up to see Maine looking out the window. He quickly gets in the car as Maine disappears from the window.

                    RICH
          What an idiot.

Rich hot-wires the car and drives off. He flips through the radio, landing on a heavy metal station.

He drives around, coming to a stop in front of the First National Bank.

                    RICH
          Let's see what you got.

Rich gets out of the car, walks over to the bank, and looks around. He checks the various cameras, and spots all the doors. He checks his watch, "11:07".

                    RICH
          Seven more hours.

He heads back towards the car, grabs the large black back pack out of the car and continues to a convenience store on the other side of the street.

INT. CONVENIENCE STORE - CONTINUOUS

The bell rings as Rich passes through the door, causing the CLERK to take notice. The clerk, mid 30's, Indian, keeps an eye on Rich the entire time.

Rich walks over to the soda dispenser and fills an enormous cup with soda. He grabs a bag of chips, a magazine, and walks over to the counter.

                    RICH
          What's your problem Gandhi?

                    CLERK
          I am no Gandhi sir, and what do you
          mean, what is my problem?

                    RICH
          Just ring me up bitch.

                    CLERK
          I am not your bitch you asshole.
          Your bitch is waiting for me at my
          house.

Rich, furious, reaches across the counter.

                    RICH
          You fucker...

The bell rings above the door. A BEAUTIFUL WOMAN
wearing less than nothing walks in and over to the
ice cream. Both men stare with mouths open.

The clerk rings up the merchandise, while both
stare. Rich pays and they both watch in silence. The
clerk breaks the silence.

                    CLERK
          Now that's a bitch.

Rich turns and smiles.

                    RICH
          Ha! Hell yeah.

They pound fists, then Rich stuffs his purchases
into the backpack and walks out.

Rich pulls out his cell phone and dials.

                    RICH
          Hey, I found a way to get the
          money.

INT. CAR - MOMENTS LATER

Rich sits in the car reading the magazine. He
reaches for the radio and turns it to an easy
listening station. The clock reads "11:54". He pulls
a blanket out of the backpack.

Rich sips from the straw and the drink line slowly
lowers to the bottom of the glass until it is gone.

He reaches over to the radio and changes it back to
heavy metal. The clock reads "5:57". Rich puts the
car in gear and pulls it around to the back of the
bank.

He leaves the car running and gets out. The two
gangsters from before approach him.

                    GANGSTER 1
          Yo Rich what's up?

                    RICH
          My dick. For your mother.

The other gangster laughs.

                    GANGSTER 1
          Shut up bitches, I'll fuck you up.

                    RICH
          Hey easy, easy. The target is here.

A new BMW pulls into the back of the bank and into a
space marked "Bank Manager". The car shuts off and
WHITEY, white, 60's, gets out, as the gangsters walk
over to him.

The gangsters brandish their guns and surround
Whitey.

                    RICH
          Cooperate pops, and you'll live.

                    WHITEY
          Are you here for Uncle Fester?

                    RICH
          Uh, yeah. So, take us inside.

Whitey leads them to the door and unlocks it.

                    WHITEY
          Where is Captain Bosley?

                    RICH
          Sick.

                    WHITEY
          Oh. You guys are here early.

                         RICH
              Yeah, well I got a plane to catch.

The gangsters laugh. Whitey opens the door and they
enter...

INT. BANK - CONTINUOUS

They walk towards the vault.

                         RICH
              Hurry up and open it.

Whitey fumbles through his pocket and pulls out a
sheet of paper and uses it on the combination lock.

The gangsters huddle around as Whitey unlocks and
opens three more doors.

He opens the last door. The men stare in awe at the
large quantity of money.

                         GANGSTER 1
              Holy shit!

                         GANGSTER 2
              That's like twenty million dollars!

                         RICH
              Or twenty million fucks with your
              girl.

                         GANGSTER 2
              Man, fuck you.

                         GANGSTER 1
              He's right you know.

Whitey laughs and the Gangsters turn towards him.

                    GANGSTER 2
          Fuck you gramps.

Gangster 2 walks over towards Whitey, who backs up.
Rich grabs Gangster 2.

                    RICH
          Ha ha, calm your ass down and bag
          the money.

One of the gangsters pulls a handful of burlap sacks
from inside his baggy pants and throws them on the
floor.

                    RICH
          How many bags you bring?

                    GANGSTER 1
          Twenty.

The gangsters stuff the cash into the bags. Whitey
watches patiently.

One of the gangsters puts a handful of cash into his
pocket.

                    RICH
          Put it all in the bag bitch. We get
          our cut later.

                    GANGSTER 2
          They ain't gonna notice.

                    RICH
          And if they do? You wanna deal with
          Fester, go ahead.

The gangster pulls the money out of his pocket and
puts it in a bag. They fill all the bags and head
for the door.

                    RICH
          Alright, let's go.

Whitey follows.

                    WHITEY
          When do I get my share?

                    RICH
          That's not up to me gramps.

Rich turns as they exit.

                    RICH
          Shouldn't you be locking up and
          erasing the tapes or something?

                    WHITEY
          Oh yeah.

Whitey returns to the vault and locks up.

EXT. BANK - CONTINUOUS

The gangsters walk over to the idling car and throw
the bags into the back of the car. Rich stuffs two
of the bags into his black bag.

                    GANGSTER 2
          What are you doing?

                    RICH
          Making sure our slice of the pie is
          separate. Just in case Measles
          tries to short change us.

                    GANGSTER 1
          Damn Rich, you're like a fucking
          pro or something.

                    RICH
          What can I say? I'm just talented
          that way.

                    GANGSTER 1
          You sure you ain't with the mob. I
          mean, you ain't gonna skip out on
          us. Cuz I'd find you and...

                    RICH
          Bitch, we known each other for like
          ten years. What the fuck are you
          talking about?

                    GANGSTER 1
          Nothin Rich, it's just with that
          whole plane thing.

                    GANGSTER 2
          Man shut up you little bitch. You
          sound like a girl. Rich ain't goin
          nowhere, right?

                    RICH
          Where the fuck would I go?
                    (beat)
          I gotta take this cash to Measles,
          and I'll be back at the warehouse
          tonight with our cut.

Rich reaches out and grabs Gangster 1's chest.

                    RICH
          You gonna be able to buy your girl
          some tits.

Gangster 1 slaps Rich's hand away.

                    RICH
          Get the fuck outa here.

The gangsters run away as Rich gets into the car and
puts it in gear. He turns up the heavy metal music
and pulls away.

As he drives off, three unmarked police cars pull up
to the back of the bank.

INT. CAR - MOMENTS LATER

Rich speeds down Santa Monica. He pulls out his
phone from his pocket and dials.

                    VOICE   (V.O.)
          Hel...

                    RICH
          I got the money. Just like we
          planned. Now it's your turn.

Rich hangs up the phone and grows uncomfortable. He
shifts around in his seat and eyes the large empty
soda cup, next to a bag of money on the seat next to
him.

                    RICH
          Fucking Mountain Dew.

Rich removes his wallet, unbuttons his pants and
adjusts his crotch to ease some of the pressure.

                    RICH
          Damn it!

The car passes the Starbucks as Maine storms out.
Rich drives a couple more blocks, makes a turn and
screeches to a halt.

He jumps out of the car, leaving it running, and
runs over to a nook in the building next to him. A
full stream of urine hits the wall.

                    RICH
          Ahhhhh...

He relaxes and places his head against the wall.
Suddenly, the car peels out behind him and he turns.

                    RICH
          Oh shit!

Rich runs after the car, to no avail.

                    RICH
          Wait!! Come back. Damn it!

He stops when the car turns the corner. Rich looks
down at the small wet spot on his pants.

                    RICH
          Fucking genius.

He zips up and walks away. He takes out his cell
phone and dials.

                    MEASLES (V.O.)
          Hello?

                    RICH
          Measles, it's Rich.

                    MEASLES (V.O.)
          And?

                    RICH
          Someone stole the car the money was
          in.

                    MEASLES (V.O.)
          What?! How the fuck does that
          happen?

                    RICH
          I had to piss.

                    MEASLES (V.O.)
          Listen to me you little shit. You
          better get that fucking money back,
          or else you are a fucking dead man.

And I will personally deliver your dead body to your
family. You understand?

                         RICH
               I'll get all my guys on it.

Measles hangs up. The three unmarked police cars
from the bank speed past Rich.

Rich walks back to the nook where he peed and next
to the wet spot is his black bag. He picks it up and
walks towards the main road. He dials his phone
again.

                    GANGSTER 1 (V.O.)
               Yo.

                         RICH
               Listen up. Someone stole the car
               with the money before I could get
               it to Measles.

                    GANGSTER 1 (V.O.)
               Shit! How did that happen?!

                         RICH
               Never mind that! Call everyone and
               get them on the lookout for that
               fucking car!

                    GANGSTER 1 (V.O.)
               Alright.

                         RICH
               Catch him. Don't kill him. That
               little bitch is mine.

Rich hangs up the phone and places it back in his
pocket. He looks back down at his pee-soaked pants.

                         RICH
               Fucking genius.

He reaches the main street and walks awkwardly to
the bus stop. After a few seconds the bus shows up.
Rich walks on.

INT. CAR - DAY

Maine drives his car. Megan sits next to him biting
her nails.

Maine weaves in and out of the traffic, and the cars
behind him follow suit. Downtown L.A. is straight
ahead.

He drives through the maze that is Downtown LA, and
the cars scatter through all the streets crossing
each other.

Maine's cell phone rings. He picks it up.

                    MAINE
          Hello?

                    RYLAND (V.O.)
          Hey bro. You coming?

                    MAINE
          Yeah, I'll be there. I am just a
          little preoccupied right now.

                    RYLAND (V.O.)
          What's going on?

                    MAINE
          Well, Megan is in the car, and we
          are kind of in the middle of some
          serious shit right now.

                    RYLAND (V.O.)
          Ha! Are you fucking serious?

                    MAINE
          Yes.

                    RYLAND (V.O.)
          Man, you gotta dump that bitch.

                    MEGAN
          Who is that?

                    MAINE
          Ryland.

                    MEGAN
          Tell your low life brother to call
          the cops. He should know them on a
          first name basis.

                    MAINE
          Shut up Megan.

Megan folds her arms and huffs back into her seat.

                    RYLAND (V.O.)
          Should I call the cops?

                    MAINE
          You wouldn't be able to tell them
          where we are.
                    (beat)
          I'll talk to you later.

                    RYLAND (V.O.)
          Hey, I left my...

Maine hangs up the phone and hands it to Megan.

                    MAINE
          Don't talk about my brother like
          that.

                    MEGAN
          I don't like him. He's trouble, and
          for all I know, he got you in this
          mess.

                    MAINE
          My brother is a good man.

                    MEGAN
          Right. Maine, he is a bad influence
          on you. Remember the street racing?
          And now look where we are, on the
          run from mobsters and gangsters,
          with millions of dollars in the
          back seat.

                    MAINE
          This is not my fault!

                    MEGAN
          Whatever.

                    MAINE
          Just call the fucking cops.

She dials.

                    OPERATOR
          Please hold.

                    MEGAN
          What?!

The phone clicks to a dial tone.

                    MEGAN
          She fucking hung up on me!

Megan stares at the phone in disbelief. She hands it
back to Maine as the car hits a pothole. The phone
falls from their hands and in between the seats.

Maine reaches down, taking his eyes of the road
briefly, and loses control. The car swerves and
Maine frantically regains control.

                    MAINE
          You fucking get it.

                    MEGAN
          Don't yell at me!

Megan fishes for the phone as Maine speeds through the streets of Downtown L.A. The plethora of cars follow closely behind.

INT. BOSLEY'S SHOWER - MORNING

Bosley stands in a shower that is too small for him. When he crouches to put his head underneath the showerhead, his knees hit the walls.

He sings Garth Brooks' "Friends in Low Places". The tile around him has hundreds of cracks in it.

> BOSLEY
> (singing)
> ...And I saw the surprise. And the fear in his eyes. When I took his glass of champagne. And I toasted to you. Said, honey, we may be through. But you'll never hear me complain.
> (beat)
> Cause I got friends in low places. Where the whiskey drowns, and the beer chases my blues away. And I'll be okay...

Bosley shifts around a bit and hits his elbow against the tile, adding another crack.

CHYRON: "BOSLEY"

INT. DONUT SHOP - NIGHT

Bosley sits at a counter with a coffee and three donuts in front of him. He breaks one donut in half, dips it into his coffee and stuffs it into his mouth.

> BOSLEY
> Fucking Day. Damn piece of shit Day.

Bosley's cell phone rings.

                    BOSLEY
          Hello?

                    UNCLE FESTER (V.O.)
          It's Nista.
                    (beat)
          First National on Santa Monica.

                    BOSLEY
          All of it?

                    UNCLE FESTER   (V.O.)
          Yes, all of it. Be at Rosemont in
          one hour.

                    BOSLEY
          Alright.

Uncle Fester hangs up and Bosley follows suit. He
checks his watch, "9:33". He takes his time dipping
the other half of the donut into his coffee and eats
it.

He takes the other two donuts, swallows them whole,
and gulps his coffee.

Bosley wipes his mouth with a napkin and lets out a
loud burp. He recoils at the bad smell.

He reaches into his pocket and pulls out a couple of
singles and leaves them on the counter as he gets
up.

                    BOSLEY
          Thank you, Lulu, you are a
          sweetheart.

LULU, a small Mexican lady whose eyes barely clear
the counter walks up to Bosley's spot.

                    LULU
          No problem officer Bosley.

Lulu pockets the tip and cleans up the mess left by Bosley. Bosley walks out the door to...

I/E. UNMARKED POLICE CAR - CONTINUOUS

Bosley walks over to the hood of the car and rubs off some bird droppings with his bare hand.

He reaches into his pocket, pulls out his keys and gets into the car.

He turns on the car, and a nice bluegrass ditty plays on the stereo. A perfect juxtaposition to Bosley's huge frame.

Bosley takes the car onto the freeway and heads out to Malibu. He passes the lavish houses that line PCH.

> BOSLEY
> Damn rich fucks. Dance around in front of a camera and you are making money for millions.
> (beat)
> What do I get? Protect these shmucks and give my own life. For what? Pocket change and a load of bullshit.

Bosley increases his speed and cruises along PCH. The car's CB comes to life.

> CB
> (crackly)
> Report of... assault, white male... alley, cross streets... eyes and tongue cut...

Bosley looks down at the CB and turns it off. He looks back up to see a car in his lane coming straight at him. He honks and quickly swerves off the road.

                         BOSLEY
                Asshole. Jesus!

Bosley sits in his car when suddenly he grabs his
stomach in pain. He gets out of the car, runs over
to the side and pukes next to the tire.

He stands up wiping his mouth and leans against the
trunk of the car.

                         BOSLEY
        Damn Lulu, what was in that coffee?

Bosley stumbles, holding his stomach and gets back
into the car. He puts the car in gear, burps again
and recoils at the smell.

The car peels out and speeds down PCH. He reaches
his destination, just past Pepperdine, and pulls
into the driveway.

A gate blocks his way, and a guard sits in a kiosk
next to the gate. The guard reads a comic book and
doesn't look up.

                         GUARD
        Need to leave your car here.

                         BOSLEY
        You gonna make me walk.

                         GUARD
        Boss' orders.

Bosley shuts off the car, opens the door, and steps
out to...

EXT. ROSEMONT - CONTINUOUS

Bosley slams the door and stares at the long walk to
the front door as the gate opens. A couple of
sprinklers water the large lawn.

Bosley walks over to a sprinkler, cups a handful of
water, and drinks it.

He swishes the last bit in his mouth as he walks and
then spits it out just before he reaches the door.

                    BOSLEY
          This better be worth it.

Bosley brings his fist up to his mouth and kisses a
ring with a cross on it.

                    BOSLEY
          Watch over me Jesus.

He rings the doorbell. A few seconds later the door
opens and Henry stands in an inviting pose.

                    HENRY
          Mista Bosley, welcome to Rosemont.
          Mista Nista is awaitin you. Please,
          follow me.

Bosley enters and Henry closes the door.

EXT. ROSEMONT - LATER

The door opens and Bosley steps out. Henry holds the
door as one of the bikini clad women walks up to
Bosley and grabs his crotch.

                    WOMAN 1
          Damn big boy. Come back any time.

The woman stands on her toes and gives Bosley a
passionate kiss. Bosley pushes her away. The woman
walks back in and Henry closes the door.

                    HENRY
          Goodnight sir.

Bosley takes a couple of steps and then does a quick celebratory dance. He walks back to his car and opens the door. The guard still has his face in his comic book.

                    GUARD
          The women are nice, aren't they?

                    BOSLEY
          Oh, hell yeah.

He turns on the car and peels out towards Santa Monica. He picks up his cell phone and dials.

                    JAMES (V.O.)
          Yes?

                    BOSLEY
          It's Bosley, round them up and meet
          me under the pier at 3:00.

                    JAMES (V.O.)
          Yes sir.

Bosley hangs up and turns up his bluegrass CD.

EXT. PIER - LATER

A group of 5 guys hang out under the dark pier and Bosley walks down the sand to join them. They are all off duty police officers.

AUSTIN, TURNER, JAMES, VALLURY, and KELSEY. All are of various ages, races and sizes.

                    BOSLEY
          Alright, simmer down fellas.

The guys quiet down and come to attention.

                    BOSLEY
          First off, Nista is only giving us
          fifteen percent. However...

                    VALLURY
          What? That's bullshit.

                    BOSLEY
          However, that is still going to
          equate to about $500,000 each.

                    AUSTIN
          That means that the total is...

Austin counts on his fingers in an attempt to do the
math.

                    JAMES
          That's a shit load of money.

                    BOSLEY
          Yes.

                    VALLURY
          So, what bank?

                    BOSLEY
          First National on Santa Monica.

                    KELSEY
          Funny, that's my bank.

                    JAMES
          Did Day tell you?

                    BOSLEY
          No, but listen up. There is a lot
          of prep work that needs to be done.
          We go in 28 hours.

Austin starts to count on his fingers again.

                    BOSLEY
          You know Austin, you should try
          walking in with your kid next time
          you drop him off at school. You
          might learn something.

Austin reaches his middle finger while counting and just leaves it up for Bosley.

>   BOSLEY
>   Aright, so I have us set up to be
>   responding to a domestic dispute at
>   the target time.
>   (beat)
>   Austin, I want you to bring twenty
>   big bags. That's this many.

Bosley flashes ten fingers twice.

>   BOSLEY
>   Actually, never mind. Vallury, you
>   bring the bags.

>   VALLURY
>   Got it.

>   BOSLEY
>   I will take care of the bank.
>   (beat)
>   As long as none of you chicken out,
>   it should be the easiest money any
>   of us has ever made.

>   KELSEY
>   I won twenty bucks on a scratch
>   off.

>   BOSLEY
>   Shut up Kelsey. Alright fellas,
>   stay quiet and stay clean. See you
>   all in about 28 hours.

The guys disperse, and walk back up the beach.

EXT. BANK - LATER

Bosley stands outside of his car throwing pebbles at the bank. Whitey's BMW pulls up and into his parking space. Whitey gets out of his car.

                    BOSLEY
          Mr. McGovern?

Whitey turns to Bosley.

                    WHITEY
          Yes?

                    BOSLEY
          I am...

                    WHITEY
          I know who you are, Captain Bosley.

                    BOSLEY
          Can we talk?

Whitey walks over to Bosley. They proceed to a more
discrete corner.

                    WHITEY
          How can I help you?

                    BOSLEY
          Your bank is going to be robbed
          tomorrow morning.

                    WHITEY
          What?! Why don't you stop it?

Bosley looks around.

                    BOSLEY
          Actually, I want you to cooperate.

                    WHITEY
          What?! I will do no such...

                    BOSLEY
          One million will be yours.

Whitey shuts up.

                    BOSLEY
          Let me put it this way Mr.
          McGovern.

                    WHITEY
          Call me Whitey.

Bosley gives Whitey a confused look.

                    WHITEY
          It's my name.

                    BOSLEY
          Anyway, if you don't cooperate, you
          will have very powerful people at
          your door.
                    (beat)
          So, look at the million that you
          get as a gift.

Whitey leans against the wall at odds with himself.

                    WHITEY
          That's not really a choice. What do
          I have to do?

                    BOSLEY
          Tonight, after everyone has gone
          home, I want you to replace the
          security cameras with tapes from a
          previous day.

                    WHITEY
          Okay.

                    BOSLEY
          Then tomorrow, around 7-ish, we
          will be here. Just cooperate with
          what we say. We will be in and out
          in a half hour.

Whitey moves closer to Bosley.

                    WHITEY
          What about the missing money? I
          can't just act like it disappeared.

                    BOSLEY
          You won't need to.
                    (beat)
          At around 10, go into the vault and
          report the money stolen. I will
          make sure that I am the one who
          takes the case. I will find nothing
          but inconclusive evidence.

Whitey smiles and becomes anxious.

                    WHITEY
          Wow this is so exciting. I can't
          wait...

                    BOSLEY
          Just don't be an idiot and go about
          telling your wife or anything.

                    WHITEY
          Oh no, of course not.

Bosley grabs Whitey's shoulder and pulls him close.

                    BOSLEY
          Don't fuck this up Whitey. Or else
          it won't just be Uncle Fester
          coming after you.

Whitey realizes who he is dealing with and gets
overcome with a mixture of shock and fear.

The two men walk back towards the bank, Bosley
breaks off towards his car.

                    BOSLEY
          Whitey.

Whitey turns.

                         BOSLEY
          Just stay calm and it will all go
          well.

Whitey forces a smile and continues to the front
door. Bosley gets into his car, shakes his head and
laughs.

INT. POLICE STATION - DAY

Bosley speeds through the station to his office.

INT. BOSLEY'S OFFICE

Bosley enters his office, blocking the stenciled
name on the door. He closes the door and takes a
seat behind his desk. He yells through the door.

                         BOSLEY
          Day! In my office!

He rubs his forehead.

                         BOSLEY
               Fuck.

He opens his desk drawer and grabs a bottle of
aspirin. He throws a handful of pills down his
mouth.

There is a knock at his door and he quickly slams
the aspirin in the drawer.

                         BOSLEY
               What?

DAY, 30's, a waif of a Scotswoman, steps in. She
wears her gun proudly in her shoulder holster.

                         DAY
          You asked for me?

                    BOSLEY
          Right. I heard of an assault in an
          alley last night.
                    (beat)
          Anything come in on that?

Day is disappointed.

                    DAY
          He's here. They just brought him in
          from the hospital.
                    (beat)
          I was just about to interrogate...

                    BOSLEY
          I'll handle it.

                    DAY
          Well, I was hoping that I could.
                    (beat)
          You see. This is, was, my source.

                    BOSLEY
          Source?

                    DAY
          For the bank fund transfer.

                    BOSLEY
          Oh. We'll all the more reason I
          should interrogate. I have no ties
          to him.

                    DAY
          Yeah, but...

                    BOSLEY
          Day, I'm doing it. I will let you
          know what I get.
                    (beat)
          You call family.

Day shoots Bosley a "fuck you" look and walks out. Bosley sits a few more seconds and walks out of his office.

INT. INTERROGATION ROOM - MOMENTS LATER

Eddie rests his head on one of his arms, the other arm is by his side. He is hooked up intravenously to a bag.

Bosley walks in and places a folder on the table. He paces a couple of steps and turns to Eddie.

                    BOSLEY
          Eddie?

Eddie looks up, revealing his beaten face. His jaw is wired shut and the rest of his face is swollen, black and blue.

Bosley recoils at the sight. Eddie can barely hold his head up. Bosley regains his composure.

                    BOSLEY
          Listen, I'm sorry about what
          happened.

                    EDDIE
          grunt

                    BOSLEY
          I'll get right to it so you can get
          back to the hospital.
                    (beat)
          Do you know who did this to you?

                    EDDIE
          nods

                    BOSLEY
          Was it Uncle Fester?

                    EDDIE
          nods

                    BOSLEY
          Do you know why?

                    EDDIE
          nods

                    BOSLEY
          For information on the bank fund
          transfer?

                    EDDIE
          nods

                    BOSLEY
          At First National on Santa Monica?

Eddie hesitates, surprised by the question.

                    EDDIE
          nods

                    BOSLEY
          Don't worry, I have other sources.
          I've been tracking Uncle Fester for
          a while.
                    (beat)
          I will make sure he gets his. You
          have my word.

Eddie's cheeks tremble in an attempt to smile.

                    BOSLEY
          Do me a favor though. Don't give
          anyone else any of this
          information. Not even Day. I know
          she's your friend, but I have a
          feeling there might be people here
          with ties to Uncle Fester.

Eddie hesitates.

                    EDDIE
          nods

                    BOSLEY
          So just keep quiet.

Eddie gives Bosley the finger.

                    BOSLEY
          Oh shit, I'm sorry. I didn't mean
          that.

Bosley chuckles to himself as he exits.

INT. POLICE STATION - CONTINUOUS

As soon as Bosley steps out, he is approached by
Day.

                    DAY
          What did he say?

Bosley's chuckle turns to laughter, forcing Day to
crack a smirk.

                    DAY
          You're an ass, what did you find
          out?

                    BOSLEY
          That he was mugged.

                    DAY
          What?! Why would a mugger do that
          to him?

                    BOSLEY
          There are some sick people out...

                    DAY
          Wait a second. Eddie had his wallet
          on him when he was brought in.

                    BOSLEY
          He probably took the cash and left
          the wallet.

Day hesitates.

                    DAY
          Right. What did the mugger look
          like?

                    BOSLEY
          Now how the hell is he supposed to
          tell me that?

                    DAY
          I...I...

                    BOSLEY
          Just leave it alone and get back to
          work.

Bosley walks away and into his office.

EXT. PARKING LOT - DAWN

The sun cracks over the horizon. Bosley and three of
his comrades stand around two unmarked police cars.

Another unmarked police car pulls in to the parking
lot. James and Austin get out. Austin holds a box of
donuts.

                    AUSTIN
          We brought donuts!

                    BOSLEY
          You're late.

                    VALLURY
          Give them a break Bosley. They
          brought donuts.

All the cops attack the box of donuts.

                    BOSLEY
          Alright...

Bosley inhales his cream filled donut, leaving a white cream goatee around his mouth.

                    BOSLEY
          So, you guys will follow my car to
          the bank.

The five comrades laugh at Bosley.

                    BOSLEY
          What are you bitches cackling
          about?

Vallury leans in.

                    VALLURY
          You got boyfriend on your face.

Bosley hits Vallury's crotch. Vallury doubles over.

                    BOSLEY
          Fuck you!

The guys laugh, including Vallury. Bosley looks at his reflection in the window of the police car. He wipes the cream off and laughs.

                    BOSLEY
          Alright, alright. Let's go.

The guys jump into the three unmarked police cars and drive away.

INT. BOSLEY'S CAR - CONTINUOUS

Bosley picks up his CB and speaks into it.

                    BOSLEY
          This is Bosley, car 23. Requesting
          back up for a dispute at the corner
          of Montana and 11th.

                    VALLURY   (V.O.)
                   (through CB)
       This is Vallury, car 83 responding.

                    JAMES   (V.O.)
                   (through CB)
         James here, car 78 responding.

Bosley hangs the CB up and drives. Rich drives the
red Ford Escort by the unmarked police cars. Bosley
takes notice of the car.

The three unmarked police cars pull into the back of
the bank, surrounding Whitey's car. Whitey walks out
of the bank doors and stops abruptly when he sees
the cars with the police getting out.

                    WHITEY
         Hello officers?

Whitey notices Bosley approaching him.

                    WHITEY
         Oh hey. Didn't see you.
                   (beat)
         Your guys just left. It went like
         you planned.

                    BOSLEY
         What!? What do you mean, my guys?

                    WHITEY
         Yeah. The three guys that were just
         here.

Bosley grows irate.

                    BOSLEY
         Did they take the money?

                    WHITEY
         Of course, why wouldn't they.

62

                    BOSLEY
          Was I with them?

                    WHITEY
          What?

                    BOSLEY
          Was. I. With. Them?

                    WHITEY
          Of course not.

Bosley grabs Whitey.

                    BOSLEY
          Then why the fuck would you think
          that they were my guys?!

                    WHITEY
          Because they said they were.

Bosley throws Whitey to the ground.

                    WHITEY
          I'm sorry. I...I wondered why they
          were here so early.

                    VALLURY
          Those guys must have been tipped
          off.

                    BOSLEY
          Whitey. You better fucking know
          this. What did they leave in?

Whitey smiles as he stands.

                    WHITEY
          A beat-up red Ford Escort.

                    BOSLEY
          Damn it!

Whitey backs up.

                    BOSLEY
          I just saw that fucking car pass
          us.

                    AUSTIN
          Me too.

                    BOSLEY
          Let's go!

The cops run to their cars. Bosley pauses before he
enters his.

                    BOSLEY
          You better pray we catch them
          Whitey. Or you might end up singing
          karaoke with Elvis and Sinatra
          tonight.

Horror washes over Whitey's face and Bosley jumps
into his car.

INT. BOSLEY'S CAR - MOMENTS LATER

Bosley slams his hands on the steering wheel as he
speeds in the direction of the red Ford Escort. He
grabs his cell phone from his pocket and dials.

                    UNCLE FESTER (V.O.)
          This is Nista.

                    BOSLEY
          You better take a close look at
          your goons.

                    UNCLE FESTER (V.O.)
          Who is this?

                    BOSLEY
          It's Bosley.
                    (beat)
          Someone was tipped off on the bank.

                    UNCLE FESTER   (V.O.)
What do you mean?

                    BOSLEY
Someone stole the money before us.

                    UNCLE FESTER   (V.O.)
What?!

                    BOSLEY
They took off in a red Ford Escort.
We are in pursuit now.

                    UNCLE FESTER   (V.O.)
You better get that money Bosley,
or it won't just be your badge that
you lose.

                    BOSLEY
Don't threaten me Nista. I still
have the police force under my
control. I can put you away...

                    UNCLE FESTER   (V.O.)
Do you take me for an idiot Bosley?
I've had all of our conversations
recorded.
                    (beat)
Which way are they headed? I'm
coming after them.

                    BOSLEY
East on Wilshire, towards Downtown.

                    UNCLE FESTER   (V.O.)
I'm surrounded by fucking
incompetent shits. If I get to him
first Bosley, you won't see a dime.

                    BOSLEY
You can't...

                    UNCLE FESTER (V.O.)
               Get that fucking money!

Uncle Fester hangs up. Bosley slams his hands on the
steering wheel.

                         BOSLEY
               Fuck!!!

The unmarked police cars pass Rich standing on the
sidewalk, talking on the phone.

INT. CAR - LATER

Maine and Megan sit in uncomfortable silence. Megan
slowly begins to cry.

                         MEGAN
               I want to go home. Why did you get
               me into this?

                         MAINE
               You think I wanted this?

                         MEGAN
               You could have just pulled over.
               You still can.

                         MAINE
               No, I can't. They would kill us.

Megan cries harder.

                         MEGAN
               I want to go home.

                         MAINE
               Ugh! Will you please be quiet! I'm
               trying to figure this out.

Megan stares at Maine.

                         MEGAN
               Don't yell at me.

MAINE

I'm sorry. I'm just a little on
edge. Okay.

MEGAN

Do you really think you are the
only one? We are both in this car.

MAINE

Not that. Well yes that, but my
brother has cancer, okay. He told
me about a week ago. I've just been
dealing with a lot of stress
lately.

MEGAN

What? Are you serious?
          (beat)
And you didn't fucking tell me
this?

MAINE

I'm sorry I just...

MEGAN

You know what? Forget it. I can't
do this anymore. I can't believe
you kept that from me. How do you
expect this to work if you don't
communicate with me? I really
should have listened to my friends.
They all said I was too good for
you, and look at you. You are a
lazy, selfish person with no goals.

MAINE

You're breaking up with me?

MEGAN

Are you a fucking idiot? Yes, I'm
breaking up with you. Our
relationship is going nowhere. You
don't talk to me and you...

                    MAINE
We are in the middle of a fucking
high-speed chase; our lives are in
danger and you pick this moment in
time to break up with me? Do you
have a soul?

                    MEGAN
You know, you're right. I should
have done it months ago. Dr. Phil
says...

                    MAINE
I don't fucking care what Dr. Phil
says. I never care what he says.

                    MEGAN
He is a genius, and far more of a
man than you ever will be.

                    MAINE
You've got problems.

                    MEGAN
Oh, like I'm the one with the
problems. If you didn't...

                    MAINE
Yes, I already know. It's my fault.
Every little fucking thing in this
relationship has been my fault.
It's my fault that I actually have
to work instead of sitting on
daddy's penny. It's my fault that
my ambitions are in the artistic
world and not the corporate, and
it's my fault that you cheated on
me with that bartender.

Megan's jaw drops.

                    MAINE
          Yes, I knew about it, you whore,
          and I actually forgave you for it.
          You know why? Because I actually
          thought it was my fault. So, you
          know what? I'm sorry. I'm so
          fucking sorry. I'm sorry for
          anything I ever did. I'm sorry that
          you make me park two blocks away so
          your friends don't see me drive up
          in this car. I'm sorry I don't get
          along with your parents who do
          nothing but insult me. I'm sorry
          I'm allergic to your fucking cat.
          I'm sorry I got you into this mess,
          and I'm very sorry for what I'm
          about to do.

                    MEGAN
          What are you talking about?

Maine reaches back and grabs a small stack of money
and hands it to Megan.

                    MEGAN
          What are you doing? I knew you
          stole...

Maine slows the car down as he reaches a turn. He
unbuckles Megan's seat belt, opens her door, and
pushes her out.

                    MAINE
          Sorry!

She screams as she stumbles and rolls onto the
ground.

                    MAINE
          Run and hide, bitch!

EXT. DOWNTOWN LOS ANGELES - CONTINUOUS

                    MEGAN
          You asshole! It's over. You hear
          me! We're through!

Maine speeds off. The passenger door slams shut.

                    MEGAN
          Wait! Come back! I didn't mean
          it! I love you!

Megan runs into an alley and jumps into a trash bin
as the pursuers turn the corner. Megan goes
unnoticed.

INT. MEASLE'S BATH TUB - MORNING

Measles lays in a nice bubble bath with candles
surrounding him. He pushes a button on a remote and
a record player scratches on.

He relaxes with his eyes closed and sings along to
"Big Pimpin" by Jay-Z.

                    MEASLES
                  (singing)
          It's big pimpin baby. It's big
          pimpin, spendin G's. Feel me.
                  (beat)
          You know I thug em, fuck em, love
          em, leave em. Cause I don't fuckin
          need em. Take em out the hood, keep
          em lookin good. But I don't fuckin
          feed em. First time they fuss I'm
          breezin...

CHYRON: "MEASLES"

INT. BLACK SUV - NIGHT

Measles stares daggers at Uncle Fester. Uncle Fester
talks on a cell phone.

                    BOSLEY   (V.O.)
          Hello?

                    UNCLE FESTER
          It's Nista.
                    (beat)
          First National in Santa Monica.

                    BOSLEY   (V.O.)
          All of it?

                    UNCLE FESTER
          Yes, all of it. Be at Rosemont in
          one hour.

                    BOSLEY   (V.O.)
          Alright.

Uncle Fester hangs up the phone and hands it back to
Measles. They sit and listen to an Italian aria.
Measles puts the phone back in his pocket.

Uncle Fester opens up a small built-in refrigerator
and pulls out a bottle of champagne and two chilled
glasses.

                    UNCLE FESTER
          Have a drink with me Measles.

Uncle Fester pours two glasses and hands one to
Measles.

                    MEASLES
          You know Anthony. You didn't cut
          his ears off. All he has to do is
          listen and shake his head yes or
          no.

Uncle Fester pauses and ponders.

                    UNCLE FESTER
          Ha ha...you asshole. You should
          have told me that back there.

Uncle Fester raises his glass towards Measles.

                    UNCLE FESTER
          A toast... To a shit load of money!

                    MEASLES
          A shit load of money.

Both guys down the first glass and Uncle Fester
pours another.

                    UNCLE FESTER
          It's too bad our fathers aren't
          here to see what I've done with the
          business.

                    MEASLES
          Yeah.

                    UNCLE FESTER
          I mean, you have been a big help.
          And to think, my father didn't want
          you involved at all. But I told
          him; Measles is family, and we take
          care of family.

                    MEASLES
          Well, your father was an asshole.

Uncle Fester gets quiet and stares daggers at
Measles. His lip quivers and then he breaks out into
laughter.

                    UNCLE FESTER
          Ha ha. You bastard. But he was a
          great asshole.

Measles doesn't laugh. Uncle Fester reaches out his
glass and Measles reluctantly raises his against it.

                    UNCLE FESTER
          May good fortune find us both.

                    MEASLES
          Oh, it will definitely find me.

They drink.

INT. ROSEMONT - LATER

The six men enter the house. Henry holds the door
open. Cho walks in and fake punches Henry. He
doesn't flinch, disappointing Cho.

Cho forces a sneeze on to Henry's suit, and walks
in. The other guys walk in. Measles stops at Henry.

                    MEASLES
          Don't mind him Henry, he'll get his
          eventually.

Measles wipes Henry's suit and adjusts it.

                    HENRY
          Thank you, sir.

Measles walks away and joins the other guys, who
congregate in the front room.

                    UNCLE FESTER
          I think I'll jump in the hot tub.

Uncle Fester walks away and the guys follow. Measles
grabs Yar and pulls him aside.

                    MEASLES
          Listen man. I need to head home,
          my wife called. Says my kid is
          sick. Tell Uncle Fester I'll be
          back soon. He'll understand.

Measles leaves.

INT. MEASLE'S CAR - MOMENTS LATER

Measles drives his car down PCH. He flips the
overhead light on and fumbles through some trash and
papers on the seat next to him. He pulls out a
drawn map and opens it up in front of him.

He pays more attention to the map instead of the
road and wanders into the oncoming lane.

A car approaches quickly and Measles, blinded by the
headlights, quickly recovers and pulls back to his
lane.

The car that nearly hit him, Bosley's, swerves off
the road.

                    MEASLES
          Fucking idiot.

Measles drives to the warehouse district in Downtown
Los Angeles.

EXT. WAREHOUSE - NIGHT

Loud music pumps from the warehouse. Measles steps
out of his car and looks around at his surroundings.

Next to the entrance, a GANGSTER appears to be
having sex with a pile of trash. A girl's moan grows
in intensity, then the gangster abruptly stands up
and walks away.

Laying in the trash with her skirt around her neck
is CARLA. Carla stands up pissed off, and throws
trash at the gangster.

                    CARLA
          You asshole. Of course, you get
          yours. Dammit!

Carla pulls her skirt back down and looks at
Measles, who stares at her.

                    CARLA
           Wachu lookin at ese?

Measles snaps out of it and walks over to her.

                    MEASLES
           Who is Rich?

                    CARLA
           I ain't tellin you nothin.

Measles pulls out 3 $100 bills from his pocket and
hands it to CARLA.

                    MEASLES
           Who is Rich?

Carla's eyes light up at the sight of the money.

                    CARLA
           Looks like you are, pappi.

Measles stares at her waiting for an answer.

                    CARLA
           He wears a baby blue hat. Sits in
           the back.

Measles walks away. Carla grabs his arm as she
stuffs the money into her bra. She is still turned
on from her previous encounter in the trash.

                    CARLA
           You wanna be my boyfriend for very
           quick?

She motions towards the heap of trash. Measles
shoots her an odd look and turns towards the
entrance.

                    CARLA
           Dammit.

Measles opens the door and walks in.

INT. WAREHOUSE - CONTINUOUS

Loud hip-hop music blares over the speakers, as
loads of gangsters dance, do drugs, and sleep.

Measles walks through the door and makes his way
through the crowd. He bobs his head and walks to the
beat, a la John Travolta in "Saturday Night Fever".

Measles pushes a few people out of the way, getting
"fuck you" responses. He reaches the back of the
warehouse, where Rich sits on a throne like seat.

Rich has four women all over him. He pushes the
women off when he sees Measles.

                RICH
        Jesus old man. What the fuck are
        you doing here? You'll get yourself
        killed.

              MEASLES
        I doubt that.

                RICH
        What makes you so sure?

Rich brandishes his gun.

              MEASLES
        Because you wouldn't want to deal
        with the consequences.

Rich stares at Measles and slowly puts his gun away.

                RICH
        You're fucking Measles, aren't you?

              MEASLES
        Let's go somewhere quiet.

Rich gets up and Measles follows.

INT. COCAINE ROOM - CONTINUOUS

They walk into a back room where people snort
cocaine.

                    RICH
          Out. Now!

The people instantly scatter out of the room. Rich
closes the door then points to the table of cocaine.

                    RICH
          Help yourself.

                    MEASLES
          No.

Measles sits.

                    RICH
          Why are you here?

                    MEASLES
          I have a business deal for you.

Rich sits.

                    RICH
          So, what's the deal?

                    MEASLES
          Well not many people know that
          Uncle Fester is my cousin.

                    RICH
          No shit.

                    MEASLES
          Just listen...

Rich sits back.

EXT. SHIPYARD - NIGHT

CHYRON: "1970's"

TWO TEAMSTERS are tied up and gagged against an open
shipping crate. EIGHT GUYS in 70's suits unload the
bagged contents of the crate into a delivery truck.

> MEASLES (V.O.)
> Our fathers were in business
> together in the 70's. They were the
> Nista Brothers.

The Nista brothers appear from behind the delivery
truck. MARIO, with a mustache, and LUIGI. They
resemble the Mario Brothers. Both look over the
workers.

> MEASLES (V.O.)
> Mario and Luigi.
> (beat)
> Each brother had a son.

Two 11-year-old who resemble Uncle Fester and
Measles step out from behind the truck.

YOUNG UNCLE FESTER stands next to Mario, and YOUNG
MEASLES stands next to Luigi.

> MEASLES (V.O.)
> Mario had Anthony, or Uncle Fester.

A worker drops a bag he is transferring, spilling
the goods. Young Uncle Fester steps forward and
slaps him across his face. Mario stands proud.

> MEASLES (V.O.)
> And Luigi had me.

Young Measles anxiously tugs at his father's suit,
pointing up to the sky. Luigi looks up and zeroes in
on what his son is excited about.

A moth flies around a street light. Luigi shakes his head in disappointment.

                    MEASLES   (V.O.)
          Well, the business was to be turned
          over to Anth... Uncle Fester and I
          equally, when our fathers got too
          old.

Mario looks at Young Measles disapprovingly.

EXT. MARIO'S HOUSE - DAWN

Young Measles hugs his father.

                    MEASLES   (V.O.)
          So, one summer the brothers decided
          to take a fishing trip.

                    YOUNG MEASLES
          How long will you be gone?

Luigi looks at Mario.

                    MARIO
          A couple of days. We have some
          business matters to tend to.

Luigi leans down and whispers in Young Measles' ear.

                    LUIGI
          Be patient. Your chance will come.
          Luigi walks over to the car where
          Mario waits.

                    YOUNG MEASLES
          Hey papa...

Luigi turns.

                    LUIGI
          Yes?

                    YOUNG MEASLES
            Where are your fishing poles?

Luigi turns and looks at Mario with questioning
eyes.

                    MARIO
            We are going to buy them there.

                    YOUNG MEASLES
            Oh, okay.

Young Measles walks towards the house.

                    YOUNG MEASLES
            Papa...

                    LUIGI
            Yes?

                    YOUNG MEASLES
            Don't fall in.

Young Measles laughs as he runs in the house.

INT. LOG CABIN, LUIGI'S ROOM - NIGHT

Luigi closes his eyes and falls asleep.

                    MEASLES (V.O.)
            My dad fell asleep in the cabin
            that night.

INT. DARK BOX - MORNING

Luigi opens his eyes.

                    MEASLES (V.O.)
            That's not where he woke up.

Small drips of water fall on Luigi's face.

REVEAL

A wooden box at the bottom of a lake.

INT. COCAINE ROOM - MOMENTS LATER

Rich leans forward.

                    RICH
          That's fucked up.

                    MEASLES
          I want what's mine.

                    RICH
          Why don't you just kill him?

                    MEASLES
          It takes more than a bullet to
          bring down Uncle Fester. He has too
          many powerful people around him.
                    (beat)
          Besides, I don't just want to kill
          him. I want the fucking business.

                    RICH
          So, what do you want me to do?

Measles adjusts himself in his seat.

                    MEASLES
          Alright, listen close.
                    (beat)
          Tomorrow morning, I want you to rob
          the First National Bank on Santa
          Monica.

                    RICH
          Whoa man. We're fucked up punks
          here, maybe steal a wallet or a
          car, but we don't rob no banks. We
          ain't smart enough to pull that
          kind of shit off.

                    MEASLES
          Just shut up and fucking listen.
                    (beat)
          Uncle Fester is sending someone to
          rob it at around 7. You and your
          boys get there at 6. The banker is
          taken care of. He'll let you in.
          All you gotta do is take the money.

                    RICH
          How much am I taking?

                    MEASLES
          There should be around twenty
          mill...

                    RICH
          Holy fucking shit. How much do we
          get?

                    MEASLES
          Ten percent. So, don't fuck it up.
                    (beat)
          With that money I can bribe most of
          Uncle Fester's men, and with your
          help, we can take care of the rest.

                    RICH
          Alright. I will get my best guys on
          it.

                    MEASLES
          You try anything tricky, and I'll
          personally make sure that
          everything, everyone here is wiped
          out. You make this work, and I will
          make you a very wealthy ally.

Measles stands up and hands Rich a piece of paper.

                    MEASLES
          Call me at this number once you
          have gotten away from the bank.

Measles and Rich stand and walk out of the door.

                    MEASLES
          You can make yourself quite
          powerful and rich, Rich.

                    RICH
          Ha! Nice one.

                    MEASLES
          Wha?...oh.

Measles manages a slight smile, then progresses
through the crowd and out the door.

INT. CAR - DAY

Maine drives with his arms locked on the steering
wheel. The speedometer slowly runs up above 75
m.p.h. He drives through the downtown LA streets.

The gas gauge teeters at an eighth of a tank.

A bullet pierces through the rear window and then
through the front window. Maine swerves, surprised
by the bullet.

                    MAINE
          Holy fuck.

Maine looks over his shoulder at the barrage of cars
chasing him. He pushes the pedal to the floor,
forcing the car to shake.

He picks up his cell phone and dials three numbers.

                    OPERATOR (V.O.)
          911. What is your emergency?

INT. POLICE SHOWERS - MORNING

Day washes herself in the communal police showers.
She dances and sings to "Every Breath You Take" by
The Police. Another female officer walks in and
starts to shower.

                    DAY
                 (singing)
          Every breath you take. Every move
          you make. Every bond you break.
          Every step you take. I'll be
          watching you.

When Day reaches the line "I'll be watching you" she
points at the other officer. The officer gets scared
and runs out of the shower with shampoo still in her
hair.

                    DAY
                 (singing)
          Every single day. Every word you
          say. Every game you play. Every
          night you stay. I'll be watching
          you...

CHYRON: "DAY"

INT. BOSLEY'S OFFICE - NIGHT

Bosley sits in his chair and Day stands against the
closed door.

                    BOSLEY
          It's for his protection.

                    DAY
          How is revealing my source going to
          protect him?

                    BOSLEY
          We can keep surveillance on him.

                    DAY
          Twenty-four hours a day?
                    (beat)
          I don't think we have the money for
          that. Besides, you would be drawing
          more attention to him. You know
          Uncle Fester would get to him. He
          probably has people in the force
          listening.

Bosley grows uneasy

                    BOSLEY
          Listen, I think...

                    DAY
          I don't really care what you think
          Bosley. I'm not revealing my
          source.
                    (beat)
          Why are you so interested anyway?
          You make it seem as if you're
          wanting to rob the bank.

Bosley shifts uncomfortably.

                    BOSLEY
          Remember you are talking to your
          superior. Be careful of what
          accusations you make.

Day opens the door.

                    DAY
          Whatever. Just drop it. I'm not
          telling you my source.

Day walks out to...

INT. POLICE STATION - CONTINUOUS

Day walks over and takes a seat at her desk. She
files through some paper work. Bosley leaves his
office and walks out of the station. Day picks up
the phone.

                    EDDIE   (V.O.)
          Hello?

                    DAY
          Eddie, it's Molly. Listen, I'm
          growing a bit uneasy about your
          safety. You should probably head
          out of town until the bank transfer
          is finished.

                    EDDIE   (V.O.)
          What do you mean?

                    DAY
          Bosley asked me again who my source
          was. I just don't trust him. He
          just seems to really need to know
          your name. I would just feel better
          if you were gone for a few days.

                    EDDIE   (V.O.)
          Alright, I'll head out to my mom's.
          I just need to get some food for my
          cat, then I'll pack up and head
          out.

                    DAY
          Just keep a low profile. Call me on
          my cell in a couple of days. I'll
          let you know what's going on.

Day hangs up and packs her bag. She grabs her jacket
and heads out of the police station into the night.
The door closes behind her.

INT. POLICE STATION - DAY

Day opens the door with a bright morning light shining behind her. She walks over to her desk and sets her jacket down.

She grabs a note that had been placed on the desk. "Call St. John's Hospital - 310-555-8008 - Dr. Tatusko".

Day looks around, sits down and dials the number.

> NURSE (V.O.)
> St. John's hospital, how may I direct your call?

> DAY
> This is Lieutenant Day, may I speak with Dr. Tatusko please?

> NURSE (V.O.)
> He's expecting your call. One second please.

Hold music plays over the phone briefly.

> DR. TATUSKO (V.O.)
> Lieutenant Day, I have an Edward Bryden here. He asked me to call you.
> (beat)
> He was attacked last night.

> DAY
> Shit! Is he alright? Can I speak to him?

Dr. Tatusko hesitates.

> DR. TATUSKO (V.O.)
> Not really.

                    DAY
          Well can he be brought in?

                    DR. TATUSKO   (V.O.)
          He really should stay and be cared
          for, but he's...

                    DAY
          It's important that he is brought
          in for questioning.

                    DR. TATUSKO   (V.O.)
          As I was about to say. He's
          already on his way. He insisted.

                    DAY
          Oh. Thank you.

Day hangs up and walks over to Bosley's office. It's
empty, and the lights are off.

                    DAY
          Fuck.

Day walks over to the dispatch room and pokes her
head in.

                    DAY
          If any reports of a bank robbery
          come in. I want you to tell me
          immediately.

The OPERATOR gives Day a thumbs up and Day walks
back to her desk.

She sits down and attempts to look through some
paper work. Distraught, she gets up and walks
towards the front door.

Just as she reaches the door, she looks through the window and sees Bosley walking up the steps. Day panics and hides behind a desk as Bosley opens the door and walks into his office.

Day comes out from hiding and walks back over to the front door. An ambulance pulls up. The PASSENGER gets out and walks to the back and opens the door.

He and the NURSE that is inside the ambulance help Eddie out of the back.

                    DAY
          That was quick.

The nurse guides Eddie up the steps and the ambulance drives off. Day opens the door for them and sees Eddie's beaten face and wired shut jaw.

                    DAY
          Oh god, Eddie, I am so sorry.

Eddie reaches out for Day and Day takes his arm. She and the nurse walk Eddie back to the interrogation room. The nurse rolls an intravenous bag next to her.

                    BOSLEY (O.S.)
          Day! In my office!

Day looks up and turns to the nurse.

                    DAY
          Take him in there, I'll be right
          in.

The nurse hands Day a plastic bag and takes Eddie in to the interrogation room. Day walks over to her desk and drops the plastic bag, revealing Eddie's wallet and keys.

Day grabs a tape recorder from her drawer, sticks a tape in and grabs some duct tape. She walks in to the interrogation room.

INT. INTERROGATION ROOM - CONTINUOUS

Eddie is seated and the nurse adjusts the
intravenous bag. Day walks over and sticks the tape
recorder under the table next to Eddie.

                    DAY
          Eddie, do me a favor.

Day grabs Eddie's hand and guides it to the record
button of the tape recorder.

                    DAY
          If someone other than me comes in
          here to ask questions, I want you
          to press record okay?

                    EDDIE
          nods

Day puts her hand on Eddie's shoulder.

                    DAY
          I'm really sorry Eddie.

Day walks towards the exit.

                    DAY
          Nurse, if you could wait outside
          please. Someone will be right here.

Both the nurse and Day walk out.

INT. POLICE STATION - CONTINUOUS

The nurse waits outside the door and Day walks over
to Bosley's office. She stands briefly outside the
closed door and knocks.

The sticker name on the door reads "Captain Jason
Bosley". Day opens the door and walks in.

                    DAY
          You asked for me?

                    BOSLEY
          Right. I heard of an assault in an
          alley last night.
                    (beat)
          Anything come in on that?

Day is disappointed.

INT. POLICE STATION - LATER

Day sits at her desk tapping a pen, when she hears
the door open behind her. Day stands up and
approaches Bosley, who chuckles as he exits the
interrogation room.

                    DAY
          What did he say?

Bosley's chuckle turns to laughter, forcing Day to
crack a smirk.

                    DAY
          You're an ass, what did you find
          out?

                    BOSLEY
          That he was mugged.

                    DAY
          What?! Why would a mugger do that
          to him?

                    BOSLEY
          There are some sick people out...

                    DAY
          Wait a second. Eddie had his wallet
          on him when he was brought in.

                    BOSLEY
          He probably took the cash and left
          the wallet.

Day hesitates.

                    DAY
          Right. What did the mugger look
          like?

                    BOSLEY
          Now how the hell is he supposed to
          tell me that?

                    DAY
          I...I...

                    BOSLEY
          Just leave it alone and get back to
          work.

Bosley walks away and into his office. Day waves the
nurse in to the interrogation room and they both
walk in.

INT. INTERROGATION ROOM - CONTINUOUS

The nurse walks over to the intravenous bag and
moves it some.

                    DAY
          Well Eddie, I think you can go back
          to the hospital.

Eddie waves Day over to him and makes hand gestures
asking for a pen and paper. Day hands Eddie a pen
but doesn't have paper on her.

                    DAY
          Just write on the table.

Eddie writes a very big and messy "Bosley working
with Fester". He drops the pen on the table. Day
leans over and reads it.

                    DAY
          Shit! I knew it.
                    (beat)
          Listen, I will take you back to the
          hospital. You'll be safer there.

The nurse stands Eddie up and walks him to the door.

>   DAY
>   I'll be right out.

The nurse and Eddie walk out and day walks over to
the table. She grabs the tape recorder from under
the table and shuts it off.

>   DAY
>   Good job Eddie.

Day grabs her pen from the table and tries to wipe
off what Eddie wrote. It won't wipe off.

>   DAY
>   Fuck.

Day spits and tries rubbing the mark off. It smears,
eventually rubbing off. She places the small tape
recorder in her pocket and walks out.

INT. DAY'S CAR - LATER

Day watches as Eddie and the nurse walk into the
hospital. She drives off to her apartment.

INT. DAY'S APARTMENT - LATER

Day closes the door behind her and sets her keys on
a small table. She kicks her shoes off and walks
into the kitchen.

She takes out the tape recorder, rewinds it, and
places it on the kitchen table.

>   DAY
>   Alright Bosley, let's hear what you
>   said.

Day hits play and walks over to take out a pizza box
from the fridge. She listens as she eats.

                    BOSLEY (V.O.)
          Listen, I'm sorry about what
          happened.

Silence.

                    BOSLEY (V.O.)
          I'll get right to it.
                    (beat)
          Do you know who did this to you?

Silence.

                    BOSLEY (V.O.)
          Was it Uncle Fester?

Silence.

                    BOSLEY (V.O.)
          Do you know why?

Silence.

                    BOSLEY (V.O.)
          For information on the bank fund
          transfer?

Silence.

                    BOSLEY (V.O.)
          At First National on Santa Monica?

Silence.

                    BOSLEY (V.O.)
          Don't worry, I have other sources.
          I've been tracking Uncle Fester for
          a while.
                    (beat)
          I will make sure he gets his. You
          have my word.

Silence.

                    BOSLEY   (V.O.)
          Do me a favor though. Don't give
          anyone else any of this
          information. Not even Day. I know
          She's your friend, but I have a
          feeling there might be people here
          with ties to Uncle Fester.

Silence.

                    BOSLEY   (V.O.)
          So just keep quiet.

Silence.

                    BOSLEY   (V.O.)
          Oh shit, I'm sorry. I didn't mean
          that.

Day angrily hits stop.

                    DAY
          Mugger my ass.
                    (beat)
          Damn, I can't use any of this.

Day pauses for a moment, then rewinds the tape a
bit. She presses play, hears a blurb and then
rewinds it a bit more. She presses play again, this
time it is cued perfectly.

                    BOSLEY   (V.O.)
          For information on the bank fund
          transfer?

Silence.

                    BOSLEY   (V.O.)
          At First National on Santa Monica?

Day stops the tape again.

                    DAY
          How did he know what bank? I don't
          even know what bank. And why did he
          keep asking me, if he already knew?
                    (beat)
          Damn it Bosley!

Day puts on her shoes, sticks a piece of pizza in
her mouth, grabs the tape recorder, her keys and
runs out the door.

INT. POLICE CHIEF'S OFFICE - LATER

Day hits stop on the tape recorder, and stands in
front of Police Chief JACOBS, 70's. Jacobs sits in
an oversized chair. A CB crackles in the background.

                    DAY
          So, you see Chief Jacobs, how would
          he know what bank?

                    JACOBS
          Well Day, I hate to disappoint you,
          but he could have his own sources.

                    DAY
          Why would he press so much on
          finding out my source?

                    JACOBS
          Maybe to cross reference with his
          source. Or maybe for your source's
          protection. Obviously, your friend
          needed it.

                    DAY
          I just don't trust him chief.

                    JACOBS
          I know. I never really liked him
          either. But this tape doesn't do
          anything. He was just asking
          questions that your friend could
          answer with a nod.

                    DAY
          I guess.

                    JACOBS
          Just get home and rest, but keep me
          informed on anything new.

                    DAY
          Will do.

Day walks out of the office.

EXT. POLICE CHIEF'S OFFICE - CONTINUOUS

Day walks down some steps and to her car.

                    DAY
          Fucking Bosley. Damn piece of shit
          Bosley.

She enters her car.

INT. DAY'S APARTMENT - NIGHT/MORNING

Day lays in her bed with the tape recorder next to
her. The clock next to her bed speeds through from
9:37 p.m. to 6:29 a.m.

Day finally gets up, having not slept the entire
night. She gets dressed, straps her gun on, and
walks out the door.

INT. STARBUCKS - MORNING

Day enters the Starbucks and walks to the counter.
The BARISTA has his back to her.

                    DAY
          Can I have...

The barista turns, it's Maine. He holds one finger
up, asking her to wait.

                    DAY
          Okay, sorry.

Maine holds his cell phone to his ear as Day waits
to order.

                    MAINE
          Alright Ryland, I'm ready.

Maine hangs up the phone and places it in his pocket
as his BOSS, early 20's approaches him.

                    BOSS
          Were you just on your phone?

                    MAINE
          Yup.

                    BOSS
          Can't you see there is someone
          waiting?

                    DAY
          It's okay really.

                    BOSS
          First you show up almost 2 hours
          late. Now you are making personal
          calls on our time?

                    MAINE
          Yup.

                    BOSS
          People want their lattes here, and
          all you have to say is yup?

                    MAINE
          No.

                    DAY
          Actually, I want an espres...

                    BOSS
          Well, what else do you have to say?
          I've only heard yup. She's only
          heard yup.

The boss points to Day who steps back, not wanting
anything to do with what's happening.

                    BOSS
          So? What do you have to say?

                    MAINE
          Fuck you!

                    BOSS
          What?!

Day, stunned, chuckles. The boss looks at her. Maine
smiles at her.

                    BOSS
          You are fired. Get out of here now!

                    MAINE
          With pleasure you little shit. I'm
          glad to be out of this hellhole.

Maine walks towards the exit.

                    BOSS
          Like you could ever find a better
          job than this!

                    MAINE
          You have no idea what I might have
          waiting for me around the next
          corner. Ha!

Maine screams and pushes through the exit.

Day and the boss stare out the door.

                    BOSS
          I'm so sorry, did you say espresso?

                    DAY
          Huh? Oh yeah, thank you.

                    BOSS
          You know he used to be such a good
          employee. I don't know what
          happened?

                    DAY
          Who knows?

The boss hands Day her coffee.

INT. DAY'S CAR - MORNING

Day enters her car and places the coffee in a cup
holder. She turns the ignition and turns on the CB.
Bosley's voice resonates through the CB radio.

                    BOSLEY (V.O.)
                    (through CB)
          This is Bosley, car 23. Requesting
          backup for a dispute at the corner
          of Montana and 11th.

                    VALLURY (V.O.)
                    (through CB)
          This is Vallury, car 83 responding.

                    JAMES (V.O.)
                    (through CB)
          James here, car 78 responding.

Day looks out her windows and inspects her
surroundings. The streets are clear. She grabs her
cell phone and dials.

                    SECRETARY (V.O.)
          Chief Jacobs's office?

                    DAY
          This is Lieutenant Day. May I
          please speak with chief Jacobs.

              SECRETARY (V.O.)
Please hold.

              JACOBS (V.O.)
How can I help you Day?

              DAY
Did you happen to have your CB on?

              JACOBS (V.O.)
Yes. Why?

              DAY
Well, Bosley must be up to
something. Because I just got
coffee at the Starbucks at Montana
and 11th. There is nothing
happening here.

Day's car sits below a sign at the intersection of
Montana and 11th. A MOM pushes a stroller by Day's
car.

              JACOBS (V.O.)
You know that jackass has pissed me
off too many times.
                (beat)
You want his job.

              DAY
Really? Yes sir.

              JACOBS (V.O.)
I trust you. The job is yours. Now
do me a favor. Swing by that bank
and make sure things are on the
level.

              DAY
Yes sir.

Jacobs hangs up and Day drives off towards the bank.
After a few blocks, Day pulls into the parking lot.
She parks next to Whitey, who pukes next to his car.

Day walks to him.

>   DAY
>   Sir are you okay?

Whitey startles.

>   WHITEY
>   Huh? Oh yeah, sorry. Last night's
>   fish isn't sitting well with me.

>   DAY
>   Do you work here?

>   WHITEY
>   I do. How can I help you?

Day grabs a pack of gum from her pocket and puts a
piece in her mouth. She offers one to Whitey, who
refuses.

>   DAY
>   I insist.

Whitey blushes as he grabs a piece and puts it in
his mouth.

>   DAY
>   I'm looking for the bank manager.

>   WHITEY
>   You've got him.

>   DAY
>   Great. I'm Captain Day.

Day flashes her badge.

>   WHITEY
>   But it says lieutenant on your
>   badge.

                         DAY
              Never mind that. Just got promoted.
              Haven't had time to get a new one.

Day places her badge back in her pocket and extends
her hand. Whitey nervously shakes it.

                         WHITEY
              Whitey McGovern.

                         DAY
              So, I had a tip that said this bank
              might be the target of a robbery.
              Anything unusual...

                         WHITEY
              No ma'am, I've been here since six
              this morning. I make it a routine
              to check the tapes and the vault
              before we open.

                         DAY
              And everything is on the up and up?

Whitey shakes in his shoes and cracks a faint smile.

                         WHITEY
              Every tape, dollar, and pen are how
              it should be.

Day sense Whitey's uneasiness.

                         DAY
              Excellent. Tell you what. I'll send
              a couple of officers here to help
              keep an eye out.

                         WHITEY
              Oh, that won't be necessary. We
              have our own security.

                         DAY
              Are you sure?

                    WHITEY
          Yes, and he is actually late.

                    DAY
          Alright. Well Mr. McGovern, if
          anything happens, you call the
          station immediately okay.

Day walks back towards her car.

INT. POLICE STATION - DAY

Day brings out a box of photos and other things from
Bosley's office. She sets it down outside the door
and peels the name sticker from the door. Next to
the door is a water cooler.

Two women walk towards the water cooler. OPERATOR,
who has a headset around her neck, and SUPERVISOR.

                    SUPERVISOR
          ...yeah, the guy is probably
          delusional.

                    OPERATOR
          Hahaha, yeah.
                    (sarcastic)
          I have 20 million in my back seat,
          the world is gonna end.

Day pokes her head around, catching the last
statement.

                    DAY
          What did you just say?

The women startle.

                    OPERATOR
          Nothing, just some head case on the
          phone claiming he has 30 people
          trying to kill him.

                    SUPERVISOR
          We get calls like this every once
          in a while. Usually, some punk
          trying to prank us, not realizing
          we trace the calls.

                    DAY
          What did you say about 20...

                    OPERATOR
          Oh yeah, get this, he said he has
          20 million dollars in his back
          seat. Says it just appeared in his
          car or something.

Day storms to the dispatch room.

                    DAY
          Did you ever think that this guy
          might be telling the truth?

The Operator and Supervisor share a look and follow
Day.

                    DAY
          Patch me through to him.

The Operator flips a few switches.

INT. DISPATCH ROOM - CONTINUOUS

Day takes a seat in front of the massive switchboard
as the two women enter.

                    DAY
          Connect me to him.

The Operator removes her headset and hands it to
Day.

                    OPERATOR
          I'm telling you, he's a nut.

The Operator grabs the cord, plugs it in, and flips a switch.

                    OPERATOR
          You are just wasting your time.

Day puts the headset on and speaks into the microphone.

                    DAY
          This is officer Day. Who am I
          speaking with?

                    MAINE (V.O.)
          Maine Richter.

Day motions the operator to turn up the volume.

INT. MAINE'S SHOWER - MORNING

Maine stands in a normal shower holding a removable showerhead. He sings "Today" by the Smashing Pumpkins into the showerhead.

His bottles of shampoo and conditioners are all kids' products with cartoon caps.

                    MAINE
                    (singing)
          Today is the greatest, day I've
          ever known. Can't live for
          tomorrow, tomorrow's much too long.
          I'll burn my eyes out, before I get
          out.

CHYRON: "MAINE"

INT. STARBUCKS - MORNING

Maine holds his cell phone to his ear as Day waits to order.

                    MAINE
          Alright Ryland, I'm ready.

Maine hangs up the phone and places it in his pocket
as his boss approaches him.

                    BOSS
          Were you just on your phone?

                    MAINE
          Yup.

                    BOSS
          Can't you see there is someone
          waiting?

                    DAY
          It's okay really.

                    BOSS
          First you show up almost 2 hours
          late. Now you are making personal
          calls on our time?

                    MAINE
          Yup.

                    BOSS
          People want their lattes here, and
          all you have to say is yup?

                    MAINE
          No.

                    DAY
          Actually, I want an espres...

                    BOSS
          Well, what else do you have to say?
          I've only heard yup. She's only
          heard yup.

The boss points to Day who steps back, not wanting
anything to do with what's happening.

                    BOSS
          So? What do you have to say?

                    MAINE
          Fuck you!

                    BOSS
          What?!

Day, stunned chuckles. The boss looks at her. Maine
smiles at her.

                    BOSS
          You are fired. Get out of here now!

                    MAINE
          With pleasure you little shit. I'm
          glad to be out of this hellhole.

Maine walks towards the exit.

                    BOSS
          Like you could ever find a better
          job than this!

                    MAINE
          You have no idea what I might have
          waiting for me around the next
          corner. Ha!

Maine screams and pushes through the exit.

INT. CAR - DAY

Maine speeds in his car while he talks on his cell
phone. He swerves back and forth as a couple of
bullets pass through.

                    OPERATOR (V.O.)
          Thanks for waiting. Please state
          your emergency.

                    MAINE
          I already told you! There are about
          thirty people trying to kill me!

                    OPERATOR (V.O.)
          Oh right. Mr. Richter please remain
          calm. What is your location?

                    MAINE
          I am downtown, near the Staple's
          Center.

                    OPERATOR (V.O.)
          In a car?

                    MAINE
          Of course, in a car, Jesus!

A couple of bullets fly past Maine's head.

                    OPERATOR (V.O.)
          There's no need for an attitude
          sir.

                    MAINE
          Are you fucking serious? I'm being
          shot at here.

                    OPERATOR (V.O.)
          Sir, what is the make and license
          of the vehicle?

                    MAINE
          A red Ford Escort. License number
          MBF-427.

A brief moment of silence.

                    MAINE
          Hello?

                    OPERATOR (V.O.)
          Sir, that vehicle was reported
          stolen last night...

                    MAINE
          I know, I reported it! I stole it
          back this morning.

                    OPERATOR (V.O.)
          Well good for you sir. So how may
          we be of service?

                    MAINE
          Are you fucking kidding me? Did
          you forget that I have thirty
          people trying to kill me?

                    OPERATOR (V.O.)
          Oh right. Any idea why?

                    MAINE
          Well, when I stole the car back
          there was like fifteen bags filled
          with money in it.
                    (beat)
          I think the car was used for a
          robbery.

                    OPERATOR (V.O.)
          Well sir, I am not sure what to do.
          So, let me get one of my
          supervisors.
                    (beat)
          Please hold.

                    MAINE
          No, I don't want to ho...

The phone clicks and music plays. Maine drives past
downtown Los Angeles. The phone clicks.

                    DAY (V.O.)
          This is officer Day. Who am I
          speaking with?

                    MAINE
          Maine Richter.

                    DAY (V.O.)
          Mr. Richter, do me a favor. Look
          behind you and tell me what kind of
          cars are chasing you.

Maine looks in the rear view.

                    MAINE
          A few black SUV's, tons of gangster
          cars like in the rap videos, and it
          looks like some unmarked police
          cars.

Maine's rear view gets shot off.

                    DAY   (V.O.)
          I knew it.

                    MAINE
          What do you mean?

                    DAY   (V.O.)
          Don't worry about it.
                    (beat)
          This is what I want you to do.
          Drive back to the freeway, and get
          on the 10 heading west. When you
          get to the 405 exchange, I want you
          to get in the far left lane.
                    (beat)
          Don't slow down, don't stop. We
          should be set up.

                    MAINE
          Okay, any suggestions on how not to
          get shot?

                    DAY (V.O.)
          Keep your head down.

Day hangs up and Maine ducks his head down as he checks the cars behind him in his side mirror.

He makes a sharp turn and heads up a street where kids play on the sidewalks. A young kid jumps on a pogo stick across the street.

The kid stalls in the middle and stares at Maine as the car inches closer.

                    MAINE
          Get off the road!

Maine swerves as he frantically waves the kid off the road. The kid attempts to clear the road, but trips and falls over his pogo stick.

                    MAINE
          Damn it!

Maine slams on the brakes. He jumps out of the car and runs over to the kid.

                    MAINE
          Are you okay?

                    KID
          I think you broke my leg.

                    MAINE
          Sorry.

Maine grabs the kid by his arms and drags him to the sidewalk. He runs back to his car, as a black SUV speed closer.

                    KID
          Asshole!

Maine steps on the gas, leaving a small cloud of smoke. The SUV hits the Escort's back bumper, as the passengers of the SUV shoot at Maine.

He peeks back at the kid to confirm his safety and
doesn't notice the large wooden ramp ahead of him.
He looks forward, panics, and turns the wheel
sharply.

                    MAINE
          Shit!

The left wheels of the car hit the ramp, forcing the
car to swerve through some trashcans.

Behind him, the SUV heads directly for the ramp.
Maine checks the side-view mirror. The SUV smashes
through the wood.

Maine looks forward and sees the 10 freeway straight
ahead. He takes the on ramp and heads west.

The cars following him form a single-file line and
enter the freeway. The 10 freeway is surprisingly
barren. The cars form a pack across all the lanes.

Maine looks at the rear-view mirror, then straight
into the camera.

                    MAINE
          My name is Maine Richter, and this
          is how I became a legend.

The cars swarm around Maine, as he swerves in and
out and around the cars. Shots fly by, piercing
holes through Maine's car.

                    MAINE
          Get the fuck away from me!!

Maine manages to swerve his way back to the front of
the pack and pulls away. He creates some distance
between him and the pack. News helicopters fly
above.

Maine looks down at the gas meter and the light has turned on. A few more bullets pass through the glass, creating a hole big enough to blow Maine's hair. Maine stares at the gas gauge.

                    MAINE
          Fuck!

The 405 exchange approaches in the horizon. Maine moves the car to the left lane, when a bullet hits one of the tires.

The tire blows and the rubber sprays all over the freeway. Maine can't control the car and it slams hard into the median.

The car drives along the wall, throwing sparks off the side of the car. Sparks spray out from the blown tire as well.

                    MAINE
          Oh fuck!

A spark flies in through the shattered window and lands on Maine's arm burning his skin.

                    MAINE
          Ow, shit.

Maine pats his arm, letting go of the steering wheel. The car takes a sudden turn to the right, across all five lanes.

Maine grabs the steering wheel and recovers. The 405 overpass is directly above him. Maine's jaw drops as he looks straight ahead.

                    MAINE
          Oh fuck, fuck, fuck.

Directly in front of him is an enormous blockade of police cars. Each car has 3 police officers with guns pointing at the coming brigade.

SWAT team vans form the back barrier. Police cars are on all the overpasses.

Maine reacts and pulls the car hard left. The car turns and loses speed as it runs out of gas.

> MAINE
> Fuck, come on.

Maine rocks back and forth, slamming his chest against the steering wheel in an attempt to move the car a little further.

He manages to get the car all the way to the left lane, barely missing the last few police cars.

The car stops right at the start of the blockade against the median wall.

Day runs over to the Escort.

> DAY
> Mr. Richter, get out of the car!!

Maine tries to open the door, but it slams against the wall. He tries the passenger door but it won't budge.

> MAINE
> I can't.

Day pulls out a shotgun and aims it at Maine.

> MAINE
> What are you doing?!

> DAY
> Get your head down!

Maine ducks and Day shoots the windshield, blasting it to pieces.

> DAY
> Get out!

EXT. FREEWAY - CONTINUOUS

Maine crawls out of the front windshield. Two
officers cover him as they rush him away.

The entourage of cars that followed Maine see the
blockade and slam on their brakes.

Half the cars crash into a massive pile up. The
other half managed to stop before they hit anything.

Half the cars that stopped attempt to back up, but
about 10 police cars have now closed in behind them
and surround the group.

                    DAY
                (into megaphone)
          You are all under arrest. Lay on
          the ground with your hands over
          your heads. Don't let this turn
          ugly.

Bosley steps out of his car.

                    BOSLEY
          Day, I have this all under control.
                (beat)
          I was in pursuit of the suspect in
          the red Escort. He was seen leaving
          a bank rober...

                    DAY
          Bosley, do me a favor. Shut the
          fuck up and get your ass on the
          ground.

                    BOSLEY
          I will have your badge for that!

                    DAY
          You've got it wrong Bosley, I have
          your badge. You and your buddies
          there are no longer members of this
          police force.
                    (beat)
          You are all under arrest. Lay on
          the ground with...

Uncle Fester sticks his head out of the window of
his crashed SUV.

                    UNCLE FESTER
          Fuck you!

                    DAY
          Uncle Fester, is that you? Did
          anyone ever tell you that you have
          the voice of an angel?

Uncle Fester looks back in his SUV and sees Katz
bloodied against the steering wheel. He turns and
sees Cho next to him staring at his bloody hand.

                    UNCLE FESTER
          Cho, go shoot the megaphone out of
          that bitch's mouth.

                    CHO
          Yes sir!

Cho jumps out of the SUV and shoots at will. The
entire police force shoots back, killing Cho.

A massive shoot-out ensues, with the gangsters,
mobsters and corrupt cops shooting out at the police
that surround them.

A couple of police officers get shot, and a lot of
the group in the middle gets shot. Measles crawls
out of his crashed SUV and makes his way to Uncle
Fester's.

Measles opens the door to reveal Uncle Fester curled up in a ball.

                    UNCLE FESTER
          Measles, thank God it's you. Don't
          let me get shot.

Measles reaches up with his right hand brandishing a gun.

                    UNCLE FESTER
               What are you doing?

                    MEASLES
          Like our fathers used to say. Fear
          exposes all cowards.

Measles blasts Uncle Fester's head off.

                    MEASLES
          That's for my father you fuck ass.

Measles collapses and lays on the pavement. The middle group stops firing.

                    DAY
                 (into megaphone)
          Hold fire, hold fire!

The police stop shooting.

                    DAY
                 (into megaphone)
          Come out with your hands up. If you
          have a weapon in your hands, you
          will be shot.

A few gangsters, mobsters and corrupt cops raise their hands. One police officer accidentally shoots one of the gangsters in the leg. The gangster falls.

                    GANGSTER 1
          My hands were up you asshole.

                         OFFICER 1
          Sorry.

The police swarm around the group with guns pointed
at everyone. About 50 officers move in. News
helicopters roar above.

Maine sits in the back of an open SWAT van with a
blanket around him and drinks a Starbucks coffee. A
SWAT team member stands next to him with his machine
gun.

                         MAINE
          How do you guys always have coffee?
          Where do you get it from?

                         SWAT 1
          Well, um...

Another SWAT team member walks up.

                         SWAT 2
          Is that my coffee?!

                         SWAT 1
          Just let him have it.

                         SWAT 2
          That's the third time you've done
          that.

                         SWAT 1
          I'll pay you back.

                         SWAT 2
          You still owe me from the first
          time.

                         SWAT 1
          Just go back to your post.

SWAT 2 walks away.

                         SWAT 2
               Asshole.

Maine laughs and SWAT 1 joins in. Day approaches
Maine.

                         DAY
               Mr. Richter. I have to say that was
               amazing. You just turned over
               practically all of LA's crime.

Day stares at Maine.

                         DAY
               Do I know you?

                         MAINE
               I don't think so.

Day stares at the Starbucks cup in Maine's hand, and
tries to remember.

                         DAY
               Never mind. If you are ready, I
               would like to take you back to the
               station to fill out some papers and
               take some statements.

                         MAINE
               Sure thing.

Maine walks out of the van and follows Day to his
police car. On his way he passes SWAT 2 and hands
him the empty Starbucks cup.

                         MAINE
               Thanks.

SWAT 1 laughs. SWAT 2 turns towards him.

                         SWAT 2
               Screw you!

Maine chuckles as he gets into Day's car. Day turns the car around and exits the freeway.

                    DAY
          What was that about?

                    MAINE
          Just some stupid shit.

Maine sits back in the car and smiles.

INT. POLICE STATION - DAY

Maine looks at the reward sheets on the wall. Several mobsters and gangsters litter the wall. Day walks up to Maine.

                    DAY
          Please come in to my office.

Maine follows Day to the back of the station, to what used to be Bosley's office.

There are boxes of Bosley's belongings outside of the office, and Bosley's name has been mostly scratched off the door.

                    DAY
          Take a seat.

Day follows Maine in, but scratches some more of Bosley's name before she enters. She takes a small piece of sticker and places it on the bottom right of the "o".

The door closes, revealing that "Bosley" has cleverly been switched to "Da y".

INT. DAY'S OFFICE - CONTINUOUS

Maine sits in front of the desk and Day walks over to a filing cabinet. She opens the top drawer and pulls out a tape recorder and a new tape.

                    MAINE
          So how much was in the car?

                    DAY
          Eighteen bags. Not sure how much
          money. Maybe fifteen, twenty.

                    MAINE
          Million?

                    DAY
          Yeah, probably.

                    MAINE
          Ha, ha. Holy shit!

She sets the recorder in front of Maine, puts the
tape in, and hits play.

                    DAY
          Okay, just speak normally, don't
          worry about the tape.
                    (beat)
          Tell me about your day.

Maine shifts in his chair and leans close to the
tape recorder.

                    MAINE
          Well, I had just left work. I was
          walking home, because well, my car
          had been stolen. I called about
          that. So, as I'm walking, I spot a
          car in the corner of my eye that
          looks just like mine...

Maine leans back in his chair.

EXT. STREET - DAY

Maine stands on a corner. A half a block down is
Maine's car. He looks around, and quietly walks
towards the car.

                    MAINE
          That's my car.

No one is in the car, and the engine hums quietly.

                    MAINE
          The fucker is running.

Maine jumps into the car and speeds away.

INT. CAR - CONTINUOUS

Maine grips the steering wheel very tightly, and a
heavy metal song screams through the radio.

Maine looks in the rear-view mirror. No one is
behind him, but in the bottom of the rear-view
something catches his attention.

He turns his head to see 15 large burlap sacks with
hundred-dollar bills poking out.

                    MAINE
          Oh Fuck!

Maine looks around the rest of the car and out the
windows. He checks the rear-view and sees three
unmarked police cars approaching.

Maine starts to slow down and pull off to the side,
but changes his mind and floors it.

                    DAY   (V.O.)
          Why didn't you stop?

                    MAINE   (V.O.)
          I panicked, I wasn't sure who they
          were.

Maine takes a sharp right turn, and the three cars
speed around the corner behind him. In front of him,
a gangster car is parked next to a trash pile.

Carla and her previous partner, Gangster 1, have sex again. Gangster 1 and Carla approach climax when Maine drives by.

Gangster 1 sees Maine's car drive by and realizes that he needs to chase after it.

> GANGSTER 1
> Oh shit!

Gangster 1 finishes quickly, jumps off of Carla, and runs into his car.

> CARLA
> Oh, hell no! Get back here and finish.
> (beat)
> Asshole!

Maine drives down the street. A few more gangster cars join the unmarked police cars and gangster car that are in pursuit.

Maine weaves through traffic, when suddenly a black SUV speeds across in front of him.

> MAINE
> Holy shit!

Maine looks to the side and sees another black SUV coming right at him.

He speeds up, narrowly avoiding a collision. All the other cars swerve around.

The two SUV's slam on their brakes, reverse, and chase. A couple more SUV's turn the corner and join in.

> MAINE
> What the hell? How many fucking people are after this money?

Maine speeds through lights and dodges traffic. The cars behind him follow and swerve. Chaos occurs all around.

Up ahead, downtown Los Angeles approaches.

INT. DAY'S OFFICE - DAY

Maine leans back in the chair. Day flips through some paper work on her desk.

> MAINE
> You pretty much know the rest from there.

> DAY
> Did you know any of the people chasing you?

> MAINE
> Nope.

> DAY
> Could you identify them?

> MAINE
> They never got close enough for me to make out a face.

> DAY
> Damn. Was there anyone else that might have seen them?

Maine hesitates a second.

> MAINE
> Nope. Sorry.

There is a knock on the door.

> DAY
> Yes?

An OFFICER 2 opens the door and sticks his head in.

>   OFFICER 2
>   Sir, we had a Mr. McGovern from the
>   bank call. Said he met with Bosley
>   yesterday and wants to turn himself
>   in.

>   DAY
>   Thank you.

The officer leaves. Day shuts off the tape recorder,
and pumps her fist.

>   DAY
>   Yes!

Maine smiles. Day leans back in her chair with her
arms behind her head. She sits quietly and smiles
for a few seconds.

>   DAY
>   Well Mr. Richter, I don't know how
>   you can help us any further.
>   (beat)
>   I just need you to sign these
>   papers.

Day pushes a small stack of papers in front of
Maine.

>   DAY
>   Most of them are release forms. You
>   know, to be able to use your
>   statements in court and such.

>   MAINE
>   Alright.

Day hands Maine a pen and walks towards the door.

>   DAY
>   I'll have someone call you a taxi.

Day walks out. Maine fills out the papers. A few
seconds later, Day walks back in.

                    DAY
          Mr. Richter?
                    (beat)
          You know, we can't hold some of
          these guys for that long. Would you
          be interested in a witness
          relocation or something?

Maine signs the last paper and looks up at Day.

                    MAINE
          I can't leave LA. I have family
          here. I'll take my chances.

                    DAY
          Suit yourself.

                    MAINE
          What about the rewards?

                    DAY
          Right, the rewards. Listen, we
          can't afford to reward you
          everything that is on those sheets.

Maine holds the papers to himself. Day, frustrated,
leans in.

                    DAY
          Tell you what. I will give you
          $250,000 cash from the money in the
          bags. I will deal with the
          repercussions. I'm sure the chief
          will understand.
                    (beat)
          Does that seem fair.

Maine hands the papers to Day. They walk out.

EXT. POLICE STATION - CONTINUOUS

Maine shakes Day's hand just outside the station.

                         DAY
          You know, you'll probably become a
          legend at this station. Thanks
          again for all your help.

                       MAINE
          No problem.

Maine walks down the steps and enters a taxi.

The taxi pulls away, passing Megan a block down.

                       MAINE
          Slow up a second.

Maine looks out the window at Megan as she looks
back and forth from the wad of cash to the police
station.

She finally settles on the wad of cash, puts it in
her pocket and walks away from the station.

                       MAINE
          Okay.

Maine smiles.

INT. TAXI - MOMENTS LATER

Maine falls back into the seat as the taxi makes its
way to the 405 South. He picks up his cell phone and
dials out.

                    RYLAND (V.O.)
          Hello?

                       MAINE
          Ryland, it's Maine. Sorry it took
          so long. I'm on my way and have I
          got a story for you.

                    RYLAND   (V.O.)
          Alright. See you in a few.

Maine hangs up the phone. He relaxes in the taxi.

                    MAINE   (V.O.)
          So, the police weren't exactly sure
          how much was stolen, but they
          estimated it at about 18 million.

The taxi exits the freeway as an airplane flies
overhead.

                    MAINE   (V.O.)
          Whitey, seeing the chase and
          arrests on T.V., decided to turn
          himself in and work out a plea
          bargain.
                    (beat)
          I won't need to appear in court.
                    (beat)
          As for me...

The giant LAX sign passes outside the taxi window.

                    MAINE   (V.O.)
          Well, after I had just told the
          police that my car was stolen, I
          got a call back from my brother.

The taxi pulls up to a terminal and Maine exits.

INT. MAINE'S APARTMENT - NIGHT

Maine puts on some clothes and picks up the ringing
phone.

                    MAINE
          Hey Ryland.

                    RYLAND   (V.O.)
          Hey, I found a way to get some
          money.

                    MAINE
          Huh? What?

                    RYLAND   (V.O.)
          For my chemo you idiot. I know how
          we can get some money.

Maine sulks on his couch.

                    MAINE
          Oh, that's great man. You find a
          job?

                    RYLAND   (V.O.)
          Nah...
                    (beat)
          What the hell's wrong with you man?
          Thought you'd be happy to hear...

                    MAINE
          I am bro, don't get me wrong.
                    (beat)
          It's just that my car was stolen
          like ten minutes ago.

                    RYLAND   (V.O.)
          Well, that's part of what I'm
          trying to tell you.

                    MAINE
          What are you talking about? And why
          did you ask me about street racing?

                    RYLAND   (V.O.)
          Didn't you see who stole your car?

Maine stares at his phone, confused.

INT. AIRPORT TERMINAL - DAY

Maine walks in to a busy airport terminal and looks
around.

                    RICH (O.S.)
          Maine! Over here.

Maine looks around and spots his brother finishing
at the ticketing line.

Maine's brother Ryland is Rich, with the light blue
hat still on his head.

Maine walks over, smiling.

                    MAINE
          That was you pissing by the
          building?!

                    RICH
          Ha! Yeah. I had to go.

                    MAINE
          I thought you would have been far
          away from there.

                    RICH
          No, I had just jumped out. Did you
          get my wallet? I really had to piss
          so I jumped out quick.

                    MAINE
          Yeah, I got it. Wait did you...

                    RICH
          Yeah, I got enough. Don't worry.

                    MAINE
          I can't believe it worked

                    RICH
          What can I say? I'm just talented
          that way.

                    MAINE
          Fucker, what about me? Do you have
          any idea what I went through? I was
          on a high-speed chase through all
          of L.A.

                    RICH
          Come on, we used to do that for
          fun.

                    MAINE
          I was being shot at, you asshole.

                    RICH
          Those were fake bullets.

Maine stares at Rich.

                    RICH
          Naw, just kidding, they were real.
                    (beat)
          Hey man, relax. You're here now.

Rich picks up his large black backpack. Maine
punches Rich's arm.

                    MAINE
          That's for stealing my car you
          asshole.

Ryland punches Maine back and Maine gives him a
dirty look.

                    RICH
          What? You stole it back!

They both laugh and then embrace.

                    MAINE
                    (whisper)
          So how much...

                         RICH
               Around two million.

                         MAINE
               You fit all that in there?

     Maine motions towards Rich's back pack.

                         RICH
               Yup.

                         MAINE
               They gave me a quarter million in
               reward money.

                         RICH
               Bonus!

                         MAINE
               After all the shit I went through
               for you. I deserve it.

                         RICH
               I appreciate it.

                         MAINE
               Hell, it was fun.

     They walk towards a hallway.

                         RICH
               So, what happened with Megan?

                         MAINE
               Ha! She broke up with me. I'll tell
               you more on the plane.

     Maine smiles as a SECURITY guard approaches.

                         SECURITY
               Mr. Rich ter?

                         RICH
               It's Rick ter.

                    SECURITY
          Come with me.

Rich picks up the backpack and they follow the
Security guard. Maine gives his brother an uneasy
look. Rich throws his arm on his brother's
shoulder.

                    RICH
          Relax bro, we're VIP

Maine smiles.

                    MAINE
          So where are we going?

                    RICH
          Australia mate!

Rich and Maine follow the Security guard through a
door marked "Authorized Personnel Only". The door
slams shut.

FADE TO BLACK.

www.ingramcontent.com/pod-product-compliance
Lightning Source LLC
Chambersburg PA
CBHW062008280526
45787CB00005B/2028